MW00711352

100%

Language

Activities for Language Comprehension

Patti Halfman

Skill Area:	Language & Listening
Ages:	9 thru 14
Grades:	4 thru 9

LinguiSystems

LinguiSystems, Inc.
3100 4th Avenue
East Moline, IL 61244-9700
1-800-PRO IDEA
1-800-776-4332

FAX: 1-800-577-4555
E-mail: service@linguisystems.com
Web: www.linguisystems.com
TDD: 1-800-933-8331
(for those with hearing impairments)

ISBN 0-7606-0514-9

Shoemaker

About the Author

Patti Halfman, M.A., CCC-SLP, is a speech-language pathologist who spends her work day talking with LinguiSystems customers. Before joining the staff of LinguiSystems, Patti worked in various school settings helping children in preschool through high school.

100% Language—Intermediate is Patti's third publication with LinguiSystems. She is also the author of *100% Language—Primary* and co-author of *Scissors, Glue, and Vocabulary, Too!*

Dedication

To my children and their friends and families —
life is a wonderful journey full of experiences.
Thank you for sharing yours with me.

Illustrations by Roberta Collier-Morales
and Margaret Warner
Cover Design by Chris Claus
Page Layout by Lisa Parker

Table of Contents

Introduction

Do your students struggle with language tasks? Do they experience difficulty mastering basic language skills? If so, they are undoubtedly frustrated with our complex language. Oftentimes, older students find themselves lost in the language or feel left behind in the midst of a group engaged in general conversation. The demands of our language require us to process so much information that when we are unable to keep up, we fail to understand what is going on or being said. Because students with poor language skills don't make natural connections between what they see and know, they may not "get" knowledge that is obvious to most people or that most of us think of as just plain common sense.

Unfortunately, students who have trouble with basic language skills and just don't seem to "get" it will probably experience difficulty with self-expression, decision-making, social development, reading, and math. However, if you can intervene and help make these language tasks manageable and more automatic for your students, their road to success will be much smoother. *100% Language— Intermediate* is full of ready-to-use activities designed to help you do just that. Once your students learn these skills and begin to understand and use language more effectively, they will become more successful in other areas as well.

100% Language–Intermediate is divided into six language areas that progress in difficulty throughout each unit:

- Sequencing
- Cause & Effect
- Problem Solving
- Opinions
- Inferencing
- Paraphrasing

Each unit includes the following components:

- Overview
- Progress Chart
- 24 activity pages
- Parent/Caregiver Letter

■ Overview

The overview offers a brief description of the unit, additional suggestions for introducing the unit and using the activity pages, and expansion activities to help you provide opportunities for your students to generalize what they've learned.

■ Progress Chart

The progress chart is a tool you can use to keep track of the activities a student has completed and record any comments you might have on his performance.

■ Activity Pages

The activities are designed for one-on-one or classroom use with students ages 9-14. The pages progress in difficulty throughout each unit. Some of them contain pictures to give the student clues to the answers; however, they generally do not provide answers to the questions. The pictures may also be beneficial when working with ESL students or students who have a more limited vocabulary.

These activity pages allow the student to practice both verbal and written language situations. Many of the activity pages provide the opportunity for the student to give a written response. As students get older, written tasks are more prevalent. Students who have difficulty with general language tasks often have difficulty applying language to written tasks. Other pages are intended to be answered orally; however, you may choose to incorporate writing into these tasks by having students write their responses on a separate sheet of paper. Likewise, you may also choose to change the directions on activity pages that require the students to provide written responses and instead instruct them to respond orally.

Activities 23 and 24 in each unit are included to provide students with opportunities to apply the targeted language skills to more real-life situations.

■ Parent/Caregiver Letter

A family letter has been provided for each unit telling parents and caregivers what the child has been learning. There are also some activity ideas for family members to use to help the student continue practicing a particular skill at home.

As you work through the units in *100% Language—Intermediate*, you may notice that there are some similarities across language areas. This is because the targeted language skills are not pure in themselves, but rather, they build one upon the other. I've attempted to separate the tasks enough so that students can focus on one area of language at a time, thereby strengthening it to improve their overall language.

I hope you and your students enjoy this simple approach to improving language comprehension.

Patti

6

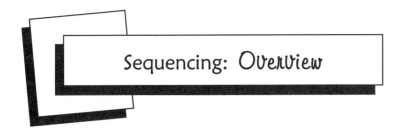

Sequencing: Overview

Sequencing is an important language skill for students to acquire. The ability to sequence impacts a student's success in areas such as following directions, reading and language comprehension, and self-expression. As your students get older, they'll need to be able to sequence quickly and efficiently to meet the demands of school requirements and everyday situations.

The activities in this unit offer your students an opportunity to practice their understanding of the language of sequencing. Activities include common sequencing vocabulary, following directions, sequencing stories and events, and understanding time concepts. They are intended to reflect the kinds of situations your students will encounter on a daily basis. You may want to remind your students to use specific sequence words as necessary.

■ Using the Activity Pages

- Before assigning these pages, you may want to review basic sequencing words like *before* and *after* with your students. These words are not covered as specific activity pages, but they are incorporated. Prior understanding is assumed. Also, if students have difficulty grasping the idea of sequencing, you may want to review some simple sequencing activities using a hands-on approach. Bring in objects for your students to sequence by size, weight, etc.

- Review the vocabulary on each page. Teach any words that are new to your students. If it is not already part of the activity, you may choose to have your students cut out sequence pictures and put them in order. Then have them tell a story about the pictures.

- Expand the activities by creating your own questions or scenarios using the same patterns presented on the activity pages.

■ Expansion Activities

- Take pictures of your students doing various activities. Later, have them put the pictures in the order they happened. Then have them tell about the activities.

- Videotape your students doing various activities. Later, watch the film without sound, and have your students create their own stories. Then have them share their stories.

- Have your students write a sequel to a story you read in class or change the ending to reflect what they think should happen next in the story.

- Use a calendar each day as you talk about the days of the week and the months of the year, and the events that are happening in your school and in your area.

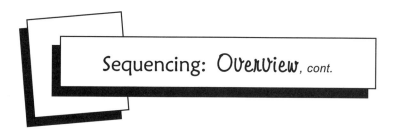

- Introduce other sequencing vocabulary like *always*, *occasionally*, *constantly*, *weekly*, and *annually* as your students are ready.

- Talk about the daily classroom schedule of events at the beginning or end of the day. Ask your students a variety of questions requiring them to sequence what will or has happened.

- When reviewing new vocabulary words for various subjects or stories you're reading, have your students practice putting the words in alphabetical order.

- Play barrier games to practice following directions.

- For students who continue to have difficulty sequencing and following directions, break information into smaller parts.

- Have students repeat directions before beginning an activity as necessary.

8

Sequencing: Progress Chart

Name _____

	Days / Trials			Comments
Activity 1				
Activity 2				
Activity 3				
Activity 4				
Activity 5				
Activity 6				
Activity 7				
Activity 8				
Activity 9				
Activity 10				
Activity 11				
Activity 12				
Activity 13				
Activity 14				
Activity 15				
Activity 16				
Activity 17				
Activity 18				
Activity 19				
Activity 20				
Activity 21				
Activity 22				
Activity 23				
Activity 24				

Name _____

Listen and follow my directions.

1. These people are buying movie tickets.
    Mark an **X** on the second person in line.

2. These children are taking turns getting
    a drink after gym class. Circle the first
    person in line.

3. These men just finished eating lunch at
    their favorite restaurant. Mark an **X** on
    the second man leaving the restaurant.

4. Point to the first bike from the door.

Name _____

Listen and follow my directions.

1. These children are waiting to have their school pictures taken. Point to the girl who is next to a boy.

2. Some children ride a school bus to school. Point to the student sitting in the last seat on the bus.

3. Joe is hungry. Point to the last thing Joe took out of the refrigerator.

4. Imagine there is a runner on first base. What is the next base he will touch?

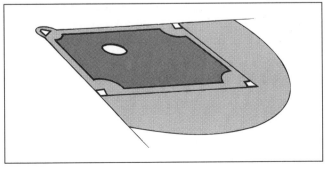

Name _____

Listen and follow my directions or answer the questions.

1. These students are running on the track during gym class. Circle the second person running. Mark an **X** on the third person. Underline the fourth person.

2. Kelsie made a necklace for her friend. She used black and white beads. Tell me the color of the third bead. Tell me the color of the fourth bead.

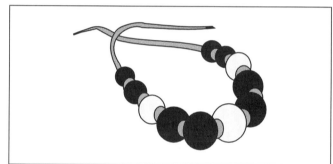

3. Phil wants to buy his sister a CD for her birthday. Tell me the price of the second CD. Tell me the price of the fourth CD.

4. These children are having fun ice skating. Circle the second child in the line. Mark an **X** on the third child.

12

Name _____

Listen and follow my directions.

1. The Millers are going fishing. Point to the first thing Mr. Miller is putting in the trunk. Name the next thing Mr. Miller will put in the trunk.

2. Mrs. Hackley needs to wash her car. Circle the item that shows the last thing she'll use.

3. The school band is marching in the parade. Point to the first row of students. Point to the next row of students. Point to the last row of students.

4. The Jefferson family is having dinner. Circle the person who will be the last to finish eating. Mark an **X** on the person who was first to finish.

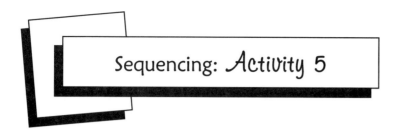

Name _____

Read each item and follow the directions.

1. Write these items in order from softest to hardest.

   leaf   rock   feather

   _____

2. Write the names of these animals in order from heaviest to lightest.

   lion   elephant   goat

   _____

3. Write these words in order from the shortest time to the longest time.

   hour   minute   day   second   year   month

   _____

4. Write the names of these items in order from fastest to slowest.

   bicycle   rocket   train   motorcycle

   _____

5. Write the names of these bodies of water in order from smallest to largest.

   lake   ocean   pond   puddle

   _____

6. Write the names of these inventions in order from oldest to newest.

   television   telephone   radio   satellite

   _____

Look at the pictures and use the small boxes to number them in the order they happened. Then use sequence words to tell the story that the pictures show.

Look at the pictures and use the small boxes to number them in the order they happened. Then draw a picture in the empty box to show what you think would happen last. Use sequence words to tell the story that the pictures show.

Sequencing: *Activity 8*

Name _____

Follow the directions.

1. Look at the bulletin board. Then write *first*, *second*, *third*, or *fourth* in each blank to complete the sentences.

   Mrs. White put some of her students' papers on the bulletin board. Later, the students looked for their papers.

   a. Corey's paper was _____.

   b. Jeff's paper was _____.

   c. Chloe's paper was _____.

   d. Adam's paper was _____.

   e. Whose paper was last? _____

2. Before Kara's mom went to work, she left Kara a list of chores she wanted her to do. Look at the note from Kara's mom. Then write what Kara is supposed to do first, second, third, and fourth on the lines below.

   Kara is supposed to do her chores in the following order:

   first _____

   second _____

   third _____

   fourth _____

Kara,

Please remember to do your chores. You need to take out the garbage, but first empty the wastebaskets. Then, wash the dishes. When you finish the dishes, please dust your room.

Thanks!
Love, Mom

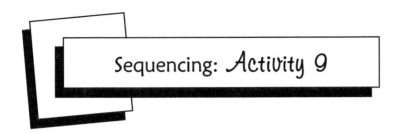

Name _____

Write *first*, *next*, or *last* in each blank to complete the sentences.

1. Mr. Clapp wants to hang a picture. The _____ thing he'll do is hammer a nail in the wall.

2. Casey wants to ride his bike, but _____ he has to put on his helmet.

3. The Jensens stayed up late watching TV. Mrs. Jensen had gotten up early that day and was tired.
    She was happy to finally go to bed. The _____ thing she did before going to sleep was turn
    out the lights.

4. Kyle was ready to call it a day. He was glad the _____ thing he had to do before going
    home was to sweep the floor.

5. Pam decided to watch a movie. First she found the movie she wanted to watch. _____,
    she turned on the TV. The _____ thing she did was put the movie into the DVD player.

6. When the florist arrived at work, she knew she needed to water the plants in the window.
    _____, she had to find the watering can. _____, she filled it with water. _____,
    she watered each plant.

7. When Danielle got home from buying groceries, the _____ thing she did was unlock the
    door. Then she took the groceries inside. _____, she unpacked the groceries. The
    _____ thing Danielle did was put away the empty bags.

8. Blair pulled into the gas station. _____, he stepped out of his car. _____, he opened
    his gas tank. Then he filled his car with gas. The _____ thing he did was go inside the gas
    station and pay for his gas.

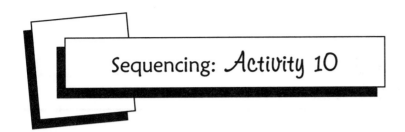

Sequencing: *Activity 10*

Name _____

Timelines show the order that events happened. Look at the timeline below. It shows the order in which some states in the U.S. joined the union. Work with a partner and practice asking and answering questions about when these states joined the union. Use sequence words in your questions and answers, such as *first*, *second*, *third*, *fourth*, *next*, and *last*.

You and your partner may even want to research some states that aren't on the timeline. Add them to the timeline in the correct order.

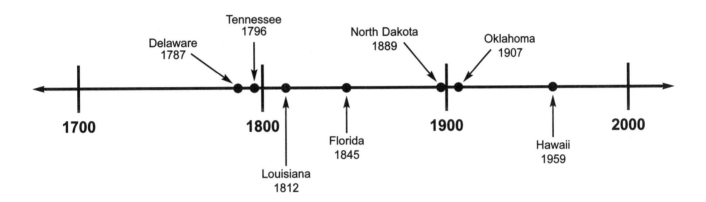

Now create a timeline showing events that have taken place in your own life or during your lifetime. Tell a friend about the events in the order they happened.

Sequencing: *Activity 11*

Name _____

Look at each task below. Number the steps in the order you would do them. Then tell how to do each task.

1. Making toast

_____ Take out a piece of bread.

_____ Put the bread in the toaster, and push the lever down.

_____ Open the bread.

_____ Put butter on the toast.

2. Putting a puzzle together

_____ Put the pieces together to make a picture.

_____ Buy the puzzle.

_____ Pour the puzzle pieces on a table.

_____ Open the box.

3. Building a fire

_____ Put the wood in the pit.

_____ Light the wood on fire.

_____ Clear the ground for a fire pit.

_____ Gather kindling and wood.

4. Planting flowers

_____ Place the dirt back into each hole around the bottom of the plant.

_____ Purchase a variety of plants.

_____ Pour water into each hole.

_____ Dig a small hole for each plant.

_____ Put one plant in each hole.

5. Washing clothes

_____ Put one load of clothes in the machine.

_____ Close the lid of the machine.

_____ Pour laundry detergent in the water.

_____ Sort the laundry.

_____ Turn the washing machine on to fill with water.

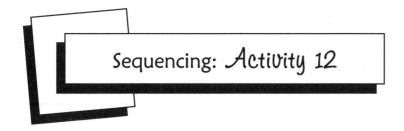
Some events happen over and over again. We call these things *cycles*. Water follows a cycle. No new water is ever made in the atmosphere. Instead, the existing water recycles again and again. The steps in the water cycle are listed below. Write the steps in the order they happen in the flow chart. The flow chart has been started for you.

• The sun's heat turns water into vapor.
• The cooled vapor changes into water droplets.
• Water falls from the clouds as rain or snow.

• The warm vapor rises and begins to cool.
• Billions of water droplets form a cloud.
• ~~Water collects in the world's bodies of water.~~

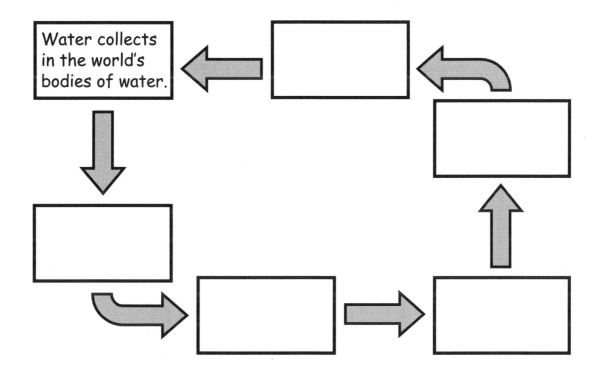

Another cycle that happens in nature is the changing of seasons. What is the order of the four seasons?

____winter____   _____   _____   _____

What other events happen in cycles?

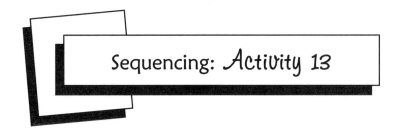

Name _____

Words have to be in order to make a complete sentence. Rewrite each set of words so the sentence is correct. If you need help getting started, remember that all sentences begin with a capital letter.

1. baby kangaroo A *joey* is called a

   _____

2. winter Bears in hibernate the

   _____

3. symbol the water is H2O for

   _____

4. do meat Vegetarians eat not

   _____

5. hope Olympic to athletes medals gold win

   _____

6. the land of the Alaska midnight sun is

   _____

7. known Chicago is City Windy as the

   _____

8. high feet is Pike's Peak 14,110

   _____

9. first walk was the Neil Armstrong moon on the astronaut to

   _____

10. studies A marine biologist live in water that animals and plants

    _____

    _____

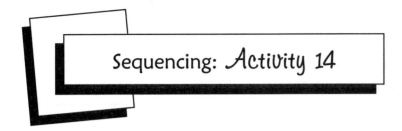

Listen and answer my questions.

1. What is the last meal of the day?

2. What is the first thing you do when you get to school?

3. When do you see movie previews?

4. What is the first meal of the day?

5. What is the first thing you do after school?

6. Are there more movie scenes after you see the words *The End*?

7. Imagine you are taking someone's food order. If the person says, ". . . and the last thing I want is a lemonade," would you need to ask that person if she wants anything else?

8. If you are supposed to clean the garage before you rake the leaves, which job will you do first?

9. If you hear an advertisement for *the last show of the season*, what do you know about the TV show?

10. Name three things you do to prepare for a test. Tell what you do first, second, and third.

11. If you could pick the next book your class reads, what would be your first choice? What would be your last choice?

12. What is the last thing you do before you turn in a final draft of a report?

13. If you did your math, then your science, and then your social studies, what did you do first? What did you do before your social studies? What did you do after you finished your math and your science?

14. Your teacher wants you to help clean the fish tank when you finish your assignment. Then she wants you to turn off all the computers that aren't being used. What does your teacher want you to do first? What will you do before you turn off the computers?

15. Ted drove a new way to work. From home, Ted turned left and went three blocks. Then he turned left again and drove five blocks. Finally, he turned right and drove two blocks. How many total turns did Ted make? How many blocks did he drive after the second turn? Which direction did he turn last?

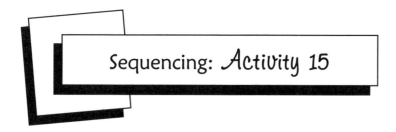

Name _____

There are many words that help us know when things happen. Listen and answer my questions. Tell me which words helped you answer the questions.

1. John's final class of the day was science.

   Was science John's first or last class of the day?

2. Following the parade, Kim went to the gas station. Then she stopped at the drugstore to pick up a prescription.

   What did Kim do first?
   What did she do second?
   What did Kim do last?

3. The initial phase of the plan is to telephone all club members.

   In this plan, are club members going to be called first or last?
   Do we know what will happen next?

4. The team looked forward to the post-game report so the players could find out what place they were in.

   Was the post-game report before or after the team played its game?

5. When Chuck got home from school, there was a message on the answering machine saying his mom had to work late and wouldn't be there to fix dinner. Chuck wasn't worried because he knew his dad would be home soon.

   Who got home first?
   Who would arrive home next?

6. Julie works until close all the time.

   Does Julie work in the morning or at night?

7. The kids were excited because they only had a half a day of school on Wednesday.

   When will the kids get out of school on Wednesday?

8. Tom starts a new job on Monday. He will help open the store every day.

   What time of day will Tom start work?

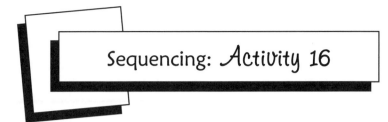

Name _____

You do many different things every day. Some things you do in a certain order. Tell the steps you would follow to do each of the activities below. Remember to use sequence words in your directions.

1. use a pay phone

2. scramble eggs

3. play your favorite card game

4. check out a library book

5. fix your favorite snack

6. make a sack lunch

7. use an elevator

8. take care of a skinned knee

9. look up a phone number

10. burn a CD

11. set an alarm clock

12. make popcorn

13. set the VCR to tape a movie

14. order pizza for delivery

15. introduce two people who don't know each other

16. get from your house to your school

17. get from your house to the nearest grocery store

18. get from your house to a friend's house

19. give someone a present

20. write a short story

Listen to each story. Next, retell the story in the order it happened. Then write what you think would happen next in each story.

A Surprise for Casey

Casey's family was moving to Utah at the end of the semester. Troy decided to plan a big going-away party for Casey. When Troy got to school in the morning, he told everyone about the party. They decided to make it a surprise for Casey. The plan was for Troy to ask Casey to come over to help him with his algebra on Saturday afternoon. The others would already be at Troy's house.

_____

_____

_____

_____

_____

_____

Born to Climb

Andrea was an adventurer. She had always loved to climb. As a young child, she climbed on the furniture at home. As she grew older, she climbed over fences and up the tallest trees. It seemed there wasn't anything she couldn't climb. By the time Andrea was in high school, she had developed a love for the mountains, too. It seemed only natural that she would combine these two loves. Andrea was only 18 when she climbed to the top of a mountain for the first time.

_____

_____

_____

_____

_____

_____

Sequencing: *Activity 18*

Stories are fun to write. Read the beginning of each story below. Then finish each story in the order you think the events would happen. Later compare your stories with your classmates' stories.

1. Krista changed clothes and went to Jessica's party. When she got there . . .

   _____

   _____

   _____

2. Clark went jogging early in the morning. While he was . . .

   _____

   _____

   _____

3. Stacey went outside to rake the leaves. After she'd raked leaves into two big piles, . . .

   _____

   _____

   _____

4. Beth tried calling her friend several times. After two hours, Beth was worried because . . .

   _____

   _____

   _____

5. Every night after Luke and his family went to bed, loud noises woke Luke up. His mom heard them, too. They both heard growling noises and what sounded like . . .

   _____

   _____

   _____

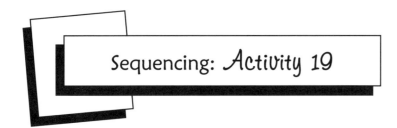

Name _____

It's important to know what time it is. Listen to each situation I describe and answer my questions.
You can use the clock to help you figure out each answer.

1. Imagine you're supposed to get up at 6:00 in the morning. If you wake up and it's 6:45 a.m., are
    you early or late?

    _____

2. Max wants to leave for the movie at 7:00 p.m. Tyler thinks they should leave at 7:30 p.m. Who
    wants to leave for the movie earlier? Who wants to leave later?

    Earlier: _____

    Later: _____

3. Joan's family is meeting at a restaurant for dinner. Joan will get there at 6:00 p.m. Her brother
    Kevin will arrive at 5:45 p.m. Joan's sister will be there at 6:30 p.m., and her parents will arrive
    at 6:15 p.m. In what order will Joan and her family arrive?

    First: _____

    Second: _____

    Third: _____

    Fourth: _____

4. Mark has a meeting at 2:00 p.m. He wants to arrive
    an hour early. What time will Mark get to his meeting?

    _____

5. Katie was going to take her mom shopping at 9:00 a.m. Katie had some problems at home and
    called her mom to tell her she'd be two hours late. What time would Katie pick up her mom?

    _____

Name _____

Look at the calendar. Let's practice using the words *today*, *tomorrow*, and *yesterday*. Listen and answer my questions.

February						
Sun	Mon	Tues	Wed	Thur	Fri	Sat
1	2	3	4	5	6	7

1. If today is Thursday, what day will it be tomorrow? What day was it yesterday?

2. If yesterday was Friday, what day is it today? What day will it be tomorrow?

3. If tomorrow is Monday, what day is it today? What day was it yesterday?

Now imagine Dan is learning to play the trumpet. He has a music lesson every Tuesday. Look at the calendar. Then listen and answer my questions.

4. Today is Tuesday. Does Dan have a lesson today?

5. Yesterday was Monday. Did Dan have a lesson yesterday? Will he have a lesson tomorrow?

6. Tomorrow is Wednesday. Does Dan have a lesson today?

7. Imagine today is Wednesday. Does Dan have a lesson today? When did he have a lesson?

8. If today were Monday, would Dan have a lesson? When would he have a lesson?

Finally, make up situations and questions of your own to ask a classmate. For example, "Kyle has to mow his neighbor's lawn on Thursday. Today is Wednesday. When does Kyle have to mow the lawn? Did Kyle mow the lawn yesterday?"

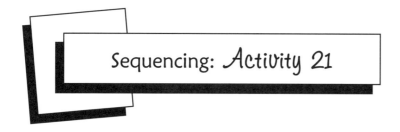
Look at the calendar. Then listen and answer my questions.

September

Sun	Mon	Tues	Wed	Thur	Fri	Sat
			1	2	3 Varsity Football Game 7:00 PM (Away)	4
5	6 Labor Day	7	8	9	10 Varsity Football Game 7:00 PM (Home)	11
12	13	14	15 Early Dismissal 1:15 PM	16 School Play 7:00 PM	17 Varsity Football Game 7:00 PM (Home)	18
19	20 Open House 6:00 to 9:00 PM Book Fair 6:00 to 8:30 PM	21	22	23 Music Festival 7:30 PM	24 Varsity Football Game 7:00 PM (Away)	25
26	27	28	29	30		

1. What holiday is in this month? Does it fall in the first half of the month or the last half?

2. What is the first school day after the holiday?

3. Which day of the week do the students have early dismissal?

4. What is happening the next day?

5. Is the Book Fair at the beginning or at the end of a week?

6. What is happening at the same time as the Book Fair?

7. Which is the last event this month?

8. Which event is first, the Music Festival or the school play?

9. What happens every Friday this month?

10. What day will the first day of the next month fall on?

Knowing the order of the months of the year is important. Many times, we have to think about their order quickly to answer a question or figure out something. Answer the questions below. Look at a calendar if you need help.

1. Write the months of the year in order. _____

    _____

2. When is your birthday? _____

3. What month was someone born in if his birthday is 12/02/86? What year was he born?

    _____

4. What month was someone born in if her birthday is 05/04/84? What year was she born?

    _____

5. If your anniversary is 10/15, what month do you celebrate your anniversary? _____

6. If your credit card expires 06/15/05, what month and year will your card expire?

    _____

7. If you have a coupon that says it's good through 04/15/08, what month and year will it expire?

    _____

8. The new school year usually starts in the eighth month of the year. What month does school

    usually start? _____

9. Spring break is usually during the third month of the year. What month would that be?

    _____

10. Summer is usually considered to be the sixth, seventh, and eighth months of the year. What are

    the names of the summer months? _____

11. If an event is held yearly, how often is the event held? _____

12. If an event is held monthly, how many times a year is the event held? _____

Name _____

Look at the advertisement for summer classes. Then answer the questions.

Summer College for Youth

Registrations must be returned no later than May 15.

Classes offered:

Sports Fitness – 9:00, 11:00, 1:00

Math (Basic Math, Algebra I, Algebra II) – all classes offered at 8:00, 1:00
* You must have passed Basic Math before taking Algebra.
* You must have completed Algebra I before taking Algebra II.

Music – 8:00, 10:00

Science – 10:00, 11:00

Computers – 9:00, 1:00

Reading – 8:00, 10:00

All classes are approximately 1 hour.

1. Today is May 15. Can Jacob register for summer classes tomorrow? _____

2. Jacob passed Basic Math, but he hasn't ever taken an algebra class. Can he still register for

   Algebra II? _____

3. Jacob wants to register for Sports Fitness, Algebra I, Music, and Computers. He can't take classes

   after 12:00. What will Jacob's schedule be? _____

   _____

4. If Jacob has to be at school at 8:00 and it takes him a half an hour to get to school, when does

   Jacob have to leave home? _____

5. If Jacob needs an hour to get ready, what time does he have to get up in the morning? _____

Write your schedule for a normal day in the calendar. Include everything from the time you get up to the time you go to bed. Then answer the questions.

Date: _____

7:00 a.m. _____	3:00 p.m. _____
8:00 a.m. _____	4:00 p.m. _____
9:00 a.m. _____	5:00 p.m. _____
10:00 a.m. _____	6:00 p.m. _____
11:00 a.m. _____	7:00 p.m. _____
12:00 p.m. _____	8:00 p.m. _____
1:00 p.m. _____	9:00 p.m. _____
2:00 p.m. _____	10:00 p.m. _____

1. Why is it important to have a schedule?

   _____

2. What things can you rearrange in your schedule?

   _____

3. What things have to stay the same in your schedule?

   _____

4. What would happen if you did things in a different order during the day?

   _____

5. Does it make a difference what day it is when you plan your schedule? Why?

   _____

6. What would change in your schedule if you had a doctor's appointment or sports practice, were sick, or went on vacation?

   _____

Dear Parent/Caregiver,

In class we've been learning how to sequence, or put things in order. You can help your child practice at home by doing activities like the ones listed below. When you do the activities with your child, remind him to use sequence words like *first*, *second*, *third*, *next*, *last*, *before*, and *after* to help him keep things in order.

- Ask your child about events that have taken place during the school day. Have him relate them in the order they happened.

- Ask your child to tell you about a TV or movie he's seen, telling the events in the order they happened.

- Ask your child to tell you how to do tasks like setting the table, doing laundry, or taking out the trash. If there are siblings, have your child teach them how to do these or other simple tasks.

- Let your child help prepare a meal. Ask him to tell you how to do each step in the right order. Use favorite recipes, or let your child choose a new recipe to follow.

- Have your child tell you about homework assignments he has and how to do them.

- Ask your child to read a newspaper article you've finished reading and tell you what has happened.

- At the end of the day, ask your child to tell you about the things he's done, keeping them in the right order.

- Use a calendar to talk about when special events will happen.

Thanks for helping your child learn!

Sincerely,

_____

Clinician

Cause & Effect: Overview

The desire to understand cause and effect begins at an early age as toddlers repeatedly ask us "Why?" Although at times this can be frustrating and exhausting to us as adults, it is an important skill for children to master. An inability to make the connection between cause and effect can have life-long implications for some children. It can have an impact on the decisions we make about what we will and won't do, give us guidelines to follow when deciding the best way to do something, and help us understand how what happens will affect others.

As children get older, applying the knowledge of cause and effect relationships may continue to be difficult. Students who have difficulty may struggle with situations that seem to be obvious to most of us. The children can't make basic inferences because they can't identify the cause and effect relationship. Understanding the premise behind general rules may not make sense to these children because they can't envision the chain of events that might occur.

The activities in this unit are designed to introduce basic cause and effect situations and provide your students with an opportunity to practice identifying and explaining cause and effect. The examples used reflect common situations and language students might encounter.

■ Using the Activity Pages

- Before beginning the activities in this unit, discuss the terms *cause* and *effect* with your students. Give some examples.

- Review the vocabulary on each page. Teach any words that may be new to your students.

- When students are working on the activity pages, you may want to write a brief definition of *cause* and *effect* on the chalkboard to serve as a reminder such as "Cause = why something happened" and "Effect = what happened."

- If your students have difficulty identifying the cause and effect relationships presented, break them apart on the chalkboard using graphic organizers.

- Expand on the ideas or situations on the activity sheets. Discuss similar situations. You may also want to introduce information that would change a particular situation, creating a different cause and effect relationship.

- Send the activity pages home for additional practice.

■ Expansion Activities

- Help your students identify cause and effect relationships in daily events. For example, what might happen if you are late to school?

- Talk about rules and why they exist. Discuss the rules you find in different places, such as at school, the ballpark, the library, home, etc., and what happens if you break the rules. Explain the cause and effect relationships.

- As you read with your students, talk about the causes and effects found throughout the stories.

- Help your students conduct some science experiments. Talk about the different causes and effects that occur.

- Discuss everyday social situations and manners that have cause and effect relationships, like why you should step to the side after getting on an elevator.

- Talk about words that signal cause and effect relationships, like *due to*, *in order*, *since*, *therefore*, *as a result*, and *consequently*. Some of these words are used in the activity sheets in this unit, but not all of them.

- Use graphic organizers to help students understand the cause and effect relationships of situations encountered in daily lessons.

- Talk about events that have both positive and negative effects, like rain. It is good for farmers' crops, but it is bad if you were planning an outdoor activity.

36

Name _____

	Days / Trials			Comments
Activity 1				
Activity 2				
Activity 3				
Activity 4				
Activity 5				
Activity 6				
Activity 7				
Activity 8				
Activity 9				
Activity 10				
Activity 11				
Activity 12				
Activity 13				
Activity 14				
Activity 15				
Activity 16				
Activity 17				
Activity 18				
Activity 19				
Activity 20				
Activity 21				
Activity 22				
Activity 23				
Activity 24				

Look at the first picture in each row.   It shows what happened.   Mark an **X** on the picture that shows why it happened.

1.

2.

Cause & Effect: Activity 2

Name _____

Look at the first picture in each row. The first picture shows what happened. Circle the picture that shows why it happened.

1.

 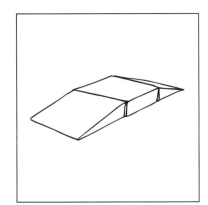 

2.

Cause & Effect: Activity 3

Name _____

Look at the first picture in each row. Tell what happened. Then circle the picture that shows why it happened. Tell why it happened.

1.

2.
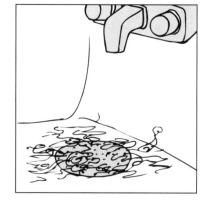

Read each situation. Then circle the letter of the correct answer.

1. What will happen if you try to pick up a cat that does not like to be held?

    a. The cat will purr softly.

    b. The cat will scratch you.

2. What will happen if you don't take care of your teeth?

    a. You will get cavities.

    b. You will have a nice smile.

3. What will happen if you break your only pencil?

    a. You won't be able to finish your math homework.

    b. You won't be able to finish reading.

4. What will happen if you don't wear shin guards when playing soccer?

    a. You won't look cool.

    b. You will get hurt.

5. What will happen if you continue to talk in the library?

    a. You will be asked to leave.

    b. You will make new friends.

Read each situation on the left. These describe things that happened (effects). Then read the situations on the right. These describe why the things happened (causes). Draw a line matching each effect to its cause.

Effects

1. The garden was beautiful.

2. The Halfmans had a wonderful dinner at Rochelle's house.

3. Daniel damaged his car backing out of a parking place.

4. Jen slid into a parked car when she slammed on the brakes.

5. Jason is afraid of dogs.

6. Fulton only likes cold pizza.

7. The fans jumped up and began clapping and whistling.

8. Carla tried to remember which stores she'd been in while she was shopping.

Causes

a. Carla couldn't find her wallet.

b. Jason was bitten by a dog when he was five years old.

c. Ryan scored a touchdown to tie the game.

d. Rochelle is a gourmet chef.

e. Fulton burned his mouth on pizza when he was little.

f. Mrs. Jackson watered her flowers every day.

g. Daniel parked too close to a pole.

h. The pavement was wet from the rain.

42

Cause & Effect: *Activity 6*

Name _____

Read each situation on the left. These describe things that happened (effects). Then read the situations on the right. These describe why the things happened (causes). Draw a line matching each effect to its cause.

Effects

1. Joe needed new shoes.

2. Sarah went shopping for a formal dress.

3. John fell asleep during the movie.

4. Kathy bought new glasses.

5. Brian's steak was too well-done.

6. Kristy had nightmares.

7. Anna jumped every time the phone rang.

8. Jeanne was disappointed after talking with her daughter.

Causes

a. The movie lasted three hours.

b. A prank caller kept calling Anna's house.

c. Blake asked Sarah to the prom.

d. The cook left the steaks on the grill too long.

e. Emily called her mom to say she wouldn't be able to meet her for dinner.

f. Kristy watched scary movies before she went to bed.

g. Joe lost one of his shoes in the lake.

h. Kathy had trouble seeing the chalkboard at school.

Cause & Effect: *Activity 7*

Listen to my questions and tell what you think might happen in each situation.

1. What might happen if you forget to give someone a message?

2. What might happen if you forget to pay your library fine?

3. What might happen if you tell a lie?

4. What might happen if you tell secrets?

5. What might happen if you don't study for a test?

6. What might happen if you turn in an assignment late?

7. What might happen if you don't do laundry?

8. What might happen if you see someone stealing and you don't tell someone in authority?

9. What might happen if someone doesn't stop smoking?

10. What might happen if you drive faster than the speed limit?

11. What might happen if you don't hit *Save* when you are typing on the computer during a storm?

12. What might happen if you don't set a timer when baking?

13. What might happen if you exercise too strenuously?

14. What might happen if you use an appliance too close to the sink?

15. What might happen if you listen to loud music all the time?

16. What might happen if the reflector on your bicycle is broken?

17. What might happen if the label on a prescription bottle is missing?

18. What might happen if the watch you're using to time a race doesn't have a second hand?

Cause & Effect: *Activity 8*

Name _____

Listen as I read each situation. Then underline what happened (the effect) and circle why it happened (the cause). The first one is done for you.

1. (Jesse grew so tall over the summer) that <u>he needed all new school clothes.</u>

2. Karen was afraid to walk alone at night because of the recent attacks on joggers.

3. Cal decided not to wash his car because the forecast called for rain.

4. Jane didn't know what time it was because she forgot her to wear her watch to the store.

5. Andy was sick on Friday, so he missed getting his math assignment.

6. Kathryn didn't look at a map before her trip and she got lost.

7. Mr. MacIntosh took his dog, Bear, to the vet because Bear wasn't eating.

8. Madison stopped eating candy and ice cream and lost ten pounds.

9. Sean felt lonely after the death of his grandfather.

10. Leah decided to clean the inside of her car so her friends would stop making fun of her.

Name _____

Listen as I read each situation (an effect). Then write a sentence telling what you think caused each thing to happen.

1. Mark said he needed to stop for gas.

   _____

2. Jill asked her mom for a snack at five o'clock, but her mom said no.

   _____

3. Todd looked outside and said he thought it would be a great day to go fishing.

   _____

4. The Franklins had to start putting their dog on a chain when it was outside.

   _____

5. Seth's mom looked outside and told him he probably wouldn't be going swimming.

   _____

6. Ramón turned on the flashlight, but nothing happened.

   _____

7. The dirt around Morgan's plant was cracked and the plant was beginning to die.

   _____

8. Mrs. Lassiter saw flowers growing in her yard that she hadn't planted.

   _____

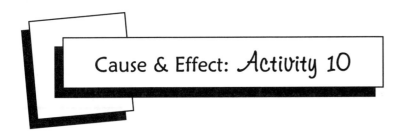

Name _____

Listen as I read each situation. Then write the cause and effect for each one.

1. If you put water in the freezer you will have ice.

   Cause: _____

   Effect: _____

2. If you drop an egg it will break.

   Cause: _____

   Effect: _____

3. Eating too much can make you sick.

   Cause: _____

   Effect: _____

4. If a large tree limb falls on your house it will damage the roof.

   Cause: _____

   Effect: _____

5. The wind blew the leaves all over the yard.

   Cause: _____

   Effect: _____

6. If you don't drink enough fluids you will become dehydrated.

   Cause: _____

   Effect: _____

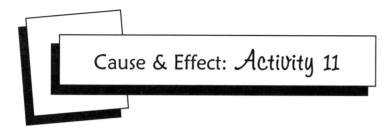

Name _____

Listen as I read each situation. Then write the cause and effect for each one.

1. School was cancelled because there was no electricity.

    Cause: _____

    Effect: _____

2. Craig's tire was flat because he ran over a nail.

    Cause: _____

    Effect: _____

3. Jarod was sad because of an argument he had with his friend.

    Cause: _____

    Effect: _____

4. Elliott was tired when he finished running.

    Cause: _____

    Effect: _____

5. Claire was in trouble because she got home late.

    Cause: _____

    Effect: _____

6. Mackenzie was glad it rained so she didn't have to water the grass.

    Cause: _____

    Effect: _____

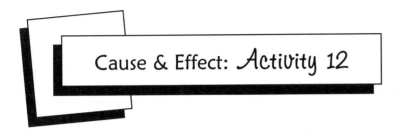
Finish the sentences by writing what might happen next in each situation. Some of the situations might have more than one possible answer.

1. If you don't get enough sleep, then _____.

2. If you don't wear shoes, then _____.

3. If you forget your glasses, then _____.

4. If you break the law, then _____.

5. If you chew gum in school, then _____.

6. If you don't take your dog for walks, then _____.

7. If you eat too much candy, then _____.

8. If you let the water run while brushing your teeth, then _____.

9. If you don't wear boots in the snow, then _____.

10. If you eat onions, then _____.

11. If you are building something and measure incorrectly, then _____.

12. If you leave a bag of garbage outside overnight, then _____.

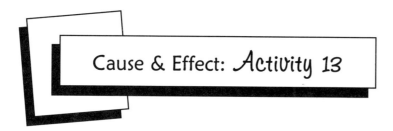

Cause & Effect: *Activity 13*

Complete the chart by writing what might happen as a result of each action.

Causes	Effects
1. telling funny jokes	
2. acting meanly	
3. littering	
4. wrestling in the house	
5. breaking the rules	
6. paying attention	
7. helping a friend with homework	
8. showing good manners	
9. volunteering	
10. playing a practical joke on someone	

Some situations can have more than one possible cause. Read each situation and write at least three reasons why it might have happened. Then think about what you would do to find out what did happen.

Effect	Possible Causes

1. The street is full of water.

   _____

   _____

   _____

2. You hear sirens outside your school.

   _____

   _____

   _____

3. When you turn on the shower, there's no hot water.

   _____

   _____

   _____

4. You can't find your favorite kind of jeans in the store.

   _____

   _____

   _____

5. When you turn on the TV, nothing happens.

   _____

   _____

   _____

The term *chain reaction* means that one event happens that causes another event to happen that causes another event, and so on. When a chain reaction occurs, what was first an effect becomes a cause. An example would be a ten-car pile up on the highway.

Read each sentence. Circle the cause and underline the effect in each sentence. Then write what might happen next. Now what is the cause and effect? The first one is done for you.

1. If (your team wins the first game) it will advance to the second round of play.

   If your team wins the second round, it will play for the championship.

2. Certain chemicals might explode if you mix them.

   _____

3. Doing nice things for people makes them happy.

   _____

4. You will be punished if you break the law.

   _____

5. Taking a hot shower relaxes you.

   _____

6. You take medicine if you are sick.

   _____

7. Eating salty foods makes you thirsty.

   _____

8. Large crowds make some people uncomfortable.

   _____

Cause & Effect: *Activity 16*

Name _____

Sometimes one event can cause many different things to happen. Think about some of the different things that could happen as a result of each item below. Then list as many effects as you can think of for each cause. When you are finished, discuss your answers with a classmate.

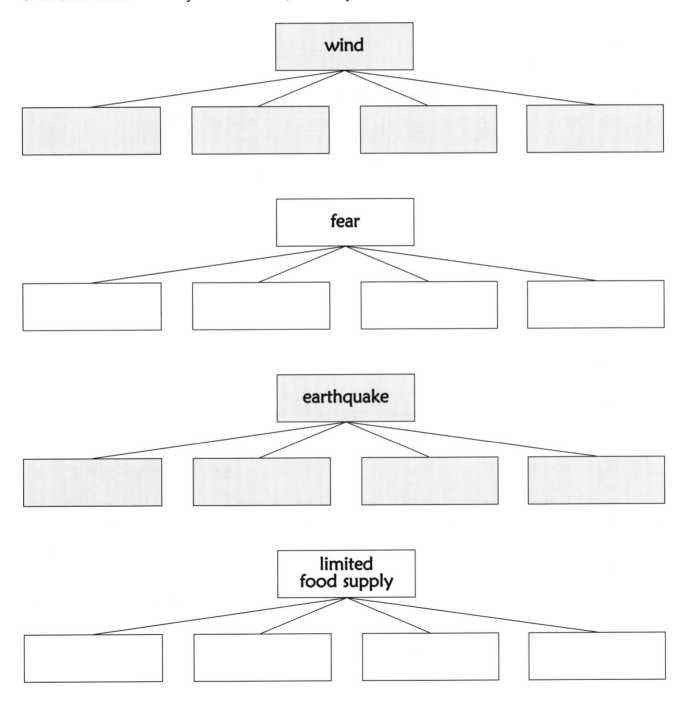

Name _____

Read each situation on the left (effects). Then read the situations on the right (causes). For each effect, write the letter of the correct cause on the line. You may need to look on the Internet, in an encyclopedia, or in your science textbook if you need help.

Effects

_____ 1. loss of habitat

_____ 2. rainbow forms

_____ 3. trees become uprooted

_____ 4. hot-air balloon flies

_____ 5. snow begins to fall

_____ 6. weather changes

_____ 7. snowflake shape is determined

_____ 8. air in clouds becomes warmer causing thunder

Causes

a. severe wind

b. change in air pressure

c. hot air rises

d. forest fires

e. lightning

f. air in clouds is below freezing

g. temperature in clouds

h. sunlight shines through raindrops

54

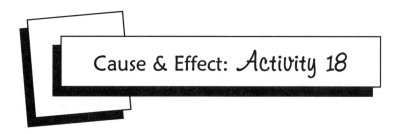

Name _____

The expression "One thing leads to another" explains the result of cause and effect relationships. One event often causes a second event that causes a third event, and so on. Look at each set of events. Rearrange the events in each set to show the ongoing cause and effect relationships. Add to each list, if you can.

1. lots of melting snow in spring, heavy snowstorms in winter, flooding

_____

_____

_____

2. use more energy, high temperatures and humidity, turn on air conditioner

_____

_____

_____

3. higher water bills, increased water use, children play outdoor sports, more laundry

_____

_____

_____

4. hot in the house, large sunny yard, cooler temperature inside, planting shade trees

_____

_____

_____

There are many organizations that serve individuals and communities in many ways. Look at the organizations below. Describe what each one does. Then identify a cause and effect associated with each organization. If you're not familiar with an organization, ask other people about it or do some research to find information.

1. *American Cancer Society*

What does this organization do? _____

_____

_____

Cause: _____

Effect: _____

2. *American Red Cross*

What does this organization do? _____

_____

_____

Cause: _____

Effect: _____

3. *Humane Society*

What does this organization do? _____

_____

_____

Cause: _____

Effect: _____

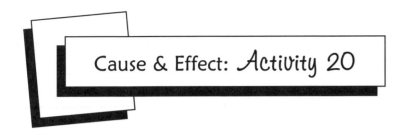

Name _____

Many things occur in nature that affect our population and our environment. Define each item below. Then list a cause and effect associated with each one. Go to the library or look on the Internet to find information to help you.

1. Greenhouse Effect

What is it? _____

_____

_____

Cause: _____

Effect: _____

2. Ultraviolet Rays

What are they? _____

_____

_____

Cause: _____

Effect: _____

3. Mirage

What is it? _____

_____

_____

Cause: _____

Effect: _____

57

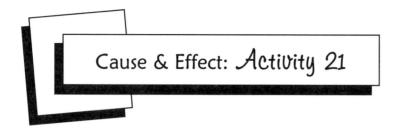

Cause & Effect: *Activity 21*

Name _____

Understanding cause and effect relationships will help you understand what you're reading. Read each paragraph. Write at least one cause and effect from each passage.

1. Clint and Joe unpacked their gear and walked to the rock wall. They prepared their equipment and began their ascent to the top. They knew when they started that it was a long route, but they wanted to try the climb anyway. As they ascended, it was harder to find incuts, so they had trouble knowing where to put their hands and feet. Finally, it became too difficult, and they had to bail. Clint and Joe both rappelled to the ground safely.

Cause: _____

Effect: _____

2. Betsy loves exploring caves. Often, she and her father go caving. Betsy's favorite kind of cave is an active cave, which is a cave with a stream in it. She thinks it's exciting to move through the cave and hear the water running over the rocks. Sometimes Betsy and her father come to places in the cave called *a squeeze*. A squeeze is a narrow passage. If the squeeze is too narrow, Betsy's father can't get through. If this happens, they have to leave the cave, or find a different way to go.

Cause: _____

Effect: _____

3. Occasionally, Betsy and her father enter a dark zone. This is an area in the cave where there isn't any daylight. Betsy and her father have to be sure they can easily reach their flashlights at all times in case they unexpectedly enter a dark zone. With their flashlights, they can continue to move safely through the cave.

Cause: _____

Effect: _____

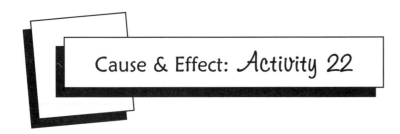

Understanding cause and effect relationships will help you understand what you're reading. Read each paragraph. Write at least one cause and effect from each passage.

1. Whitewater rafting can be an exciting adventure! When you raft, you want to be sure you have a strong and experienced guide. He is the person who will give you paddle commands to help you travel down the river safely. Before you can begin your adventure, you must take instruction on safety procedures. This is important so you know how to paddle and what to do in case of an emergency.

Cause: _____

Effect: _____

2. When rafting, you may encounter rapids. *Rapids* are places where the water flows through narrower areas of land. These areas are harder to maneuver than the rest of the river because the water is so rough. This is one time when it's important to have a good guide. It's also a good time to make sure your lifejacket is securely fastened. That's because it's easy to become a swimmer when going through a rapid. If you do fall out of the raft, your lifejacket just might save your life!

Cause: _____

Effect: _____

3. Car racing is a fascinating sport to many people. They get a thrill from just watching the speed of the cars racing around the track. A racing fan usually has a favorite driver and gets excited if this driver starts the race in pole position. This means that the driver will get to start the race on the inside of the front row of cars. A driver gets to start the race in pole position if he earns the fastest qualifying time. Pole position gives the driver a better chance of winning the race.

Cause: _____

Effect: _____

Name _____

Read the advertisement. What cause and effect relationships can you identify? Write your ideas on the lines below.

Make First-Mart your first and last stop to shop!

Broken pencils? Empty notebooks?
Shoes too small? Kids too tall?

Find all your BACK-TO-SCHOOL needs
at

First-Mart

Here when YOU need us!
Open 24 Hours

Unsure about what supplies your kids need?
We have supply lists from all local schools!
We have everything you need!

Limited budget? We have the LOWEST PRICES in town!

Cause: _____

Effect: _____

Cause: _____

Effect: _____

Cause: _____

Effect: _____

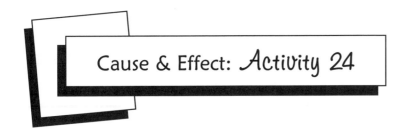

Cause & Effect: *Activity 24*

Name _____

Think about some of the events that happen every day in your life. These can include anything from a special rehearsal or practice before school to a science experiment to not feeling hungry for dinner. Each of these events has at least one cause and one effect.

Use this page to identify some of the cause and effect relationships you experience or observe throughout a day. Remember to include situations when there may be a series of causes and effects.

1. **Event:** _____

   Cause: _____

   Effect: _____

2. **Event:** _____

   Cause: _____

   Effect: _____

3. **Event:** _____

   Cause: _____

   Effect: _____

4. **Event:** _____

   Cause: _____

   Effect: _____

Dear Parent/Caregiver,

We've been talking about cause and effect relationships at school. Your child knows that the *cause* is why something happened and the *effect* is what happened. Older students don't always develop a quick understanding of why things happen. Cause and effect relationships are difficult for them to understand. Sometimes parents, teachers, and even peers become frustrated when someone doesn't understand a situation that appears to be just common sense.

You can help your child understand the concept of cause and effect relationships by discussing everyday situations. Take time to explain the "why" of things.

Some ideas to get you started are listed.

• Discuss simple situations that have cause and effect relationships, like why you wouldn't want to leave a can of pop in the freezer to get cold or what happens if you pour pop into a glass that's full of ice.

• Talk about how you know why something happened without being told. For example, you don't change a lightbulb that has just burned out because you know you'll get burned.

• Explain that rules are usually based on potential cause and effect relationships. When making rules, discuss why the rule must be in place and what will happen if it is broken.

• Talk about how someone's actions may have negative effects. For example, if you take your anger out on others, the situation will probably be worse in the long run.

Explaining these kinds of situations will help your child learn to put the pieces together more automatically in her own thinking and her language skills will be stronger.

Thanks for helping your child learn!

Sincerely,

_____

Clinician

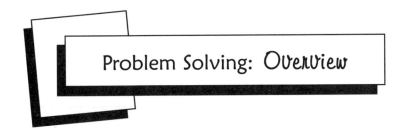

Problem Solving: Overview

This unit is designed to help your students learn to use their language skills and awareness of everyday experiences to identify, understand, solve, and avoid problems they may encounter. As your students' skills develop, they will eventually begin to apply what they've learned to their own individual situations. As students get older, the language demands increase in complexity. Students are required to think faster, process information more quickly, and respond to others more completely. Helping your students develop solid problem-solving skills will enable them to keep up with these language demands and be more successful in the classroom, at home, and in social settings.

■ Using the Activity Pages

- Review the vocabulary on each page. Teach any words that are new to your students.

- Simplify or increase the difficulty of the tasks by providing more or less information, or by rewording the directions or the questions.

- Reword questions to introduce new vocabulary. This will help your students realize that they may be asked for the same information in more than one way.

- As they complete the activity pages, encourage your students to share their own related experiences.

- Send the activity pages home for additional practice.

■ Expansion Activities

- Talk about the fact that many problems have more than one solution. Discuss how sometimes one solution may be better than another and why.

- Think of problems that may occur in your classroom, city, or town. Talk about different solutions to the problems. Then choose one of the problems and provide your students with additional information about the situation. Have them discuss whether the original solution is still the best choice or if a different solution would be better.

- As you read stories, stop periodically to talk about what problems have occurred. Ask your students to give ideas for how they would solve the problems. When you have finished reading, have your students tell you how the problem was solved in the story.

- Structure questions to give students an opportunity to think about the information they know or need to find out rather than just providing them with the facts.

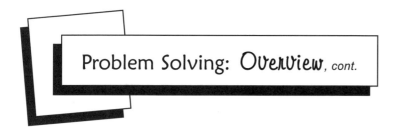

- Challenge your students to ask specific questions about information needed to complete work rather than to just say, "I don't know." Work with them to identify the problem they're having with the lesson and formulate appropriate questions.

- When a problem arises in your classroom, let your students help determine the solution. Write the situation on the chalkboard. Then have your students list possible solutions. Talk about the pros and cons of each solution. Let your students choose the solution that best fits the situation.

- Set aside time during the day to let each student tell about a problem he had or saw and how it was solved.

64

Problem Solving: Progress Chart

Name _____

	Days / Trials			Comments
Activity 1				
Activity 2				
Activity 3				
Activity 4				
Activity 5				
Activity 6				
Activity 7				
Activity 8				
Activity 9				
Activity 10				
Activity 11				
Activity 12				
Activity 13				
Activity 14				
Activity 15				
Activity 16				
Activity 17				
Activity 18				
Activity 19				
Activity 20				
Activity 21				
Activity 22				
Activity 23				
Activity 24				

Listen and then follow my directions.

1. Austin can't find his belt. Circle the picture that shows which would be better to use to hold up his pants.

2. Colleen is going to be outside all day. It is supposed to be hot and sunny. Mark an **X** on the picture that shows which would be better to use to avoid getting too much sun.

3. Ben plays on his school's baseball team. They are playing in a tournament tomorrow and their first game is at 8:00 a.m. Underline the picture that shows what Ben should do the night before the game.

66

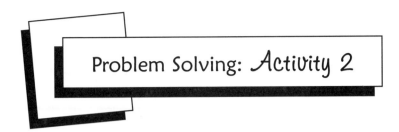

Problem Solving: *Activity 2*

Name _____

Listen and then follow my directions.

1. Anna accidentally tore a page in her science book. Underline the picture that shows which would be better to use for fixing the page.

2. Cal finished exercising and needs to get something to drink. Mark an **X** on the picture that shows which would be better for Cal to drink after exercising.

3. Mrs. Kelly lives alone and wants to get a pet to keep her company. Circle the picture that shows what kind of pet she should pick.

Name _____

Look at each picture and listen to what I say. Then tell me what the problem is.

1. The lightbulb is burned out.

2. Mrs. Cleve just received a new picture of her nephew. She's going to put it on the shelf with her other pictures.

3. The fire department is responding to a fire call in the downtown area of a busy city.

4. Brenda finished her shopping and is in a hurry to get home so the frozen foods don't thaw.

Name _____

Listen and then follow my directions.

1. Noah finished the snack he was eating and needed to get rid of the trash.   Mark an **X** on the picture that shows what Noah should do.

2. Mr. Blanchard got home very late from a trip and wanted to sleep in the next day. Early in the morning, birds chirping outside woke him up. Circle the picture that shows what Mr. Blanchard should do.

3. Tressa and her friends went to see a movie. When Tressa got to the movie theater, she realized she didn't have enough money for her ticket. Underline the picture that shows what Tressa should do.

Name _____

Look at the pictures and listen to what I say. Then answer my questions.

1. Mrs. Welch has a virus and can't go outside. What problem does she have? What should she do?

2. Kelly was driving to visit her sister at college. What problem does she have? What should she do?

3. Jack was getting ready to make dinner. What problem does Jack have? What should he do?

4. Joan loves her garden. What problem is she having? What should she do?

70

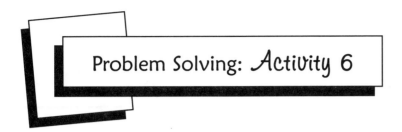

Problem Solving: Activity 6

Name _____

Read each item. Where could you look to solve each problem? Choose the correct answer from the word box and write in on the line after each item.

cookbook	**dictionary**	**newspaper**	**table of contents**
phone book	**encyclopedia**	**atlas**	**calendar**

1. You need to find a phone number.   _____

2. You need to find information on the sinking of the *Titanic*.   _____

3. You need to find the definition of a word.   _____

4. You need directions to Chicago, Illinois.   _____

5. You need to find out what page Chapter 5 of a book starts on.   _____

6. You need a recipe for Beef Wellington.   _____

7. You need to know which day of the week January 26th of next year will be.   _____

8. You need to write a paper on current events.   _____

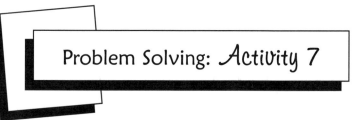

Name _____

Read each item. Where would you go or who would you call to solve each problem? Choose the correct answer from the word box and write it on the line after each item.

newspaper	**video store**	**library**	**doctor's office**
electronics store	**art gallery**	**antique store**	**police station**

1. You need some cable to hook up your stereo.　　　_____

2. You need several references for a research paper.　　　_____

3. You want to find out what time a concert is going to start.　　　_____

4. You need to report your bike stolen.　　　_____

5. You need to find out how to take care of an injury.　　　_____

6. You want to rent a DVD.　　　_____

7. You need an old desk to use in your school play.　　　_____

8. You want to see paintings by famous artists.　　　_____

Name _____

Look at each picture and tell what the problem is. Then tell what each person could do to solve the problem.

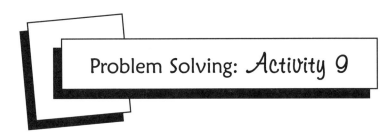

Problem Solving: Activity 9

Name _____

Look at each picture and tell what the problem is. Then tell what could have prevented the problem from happening.

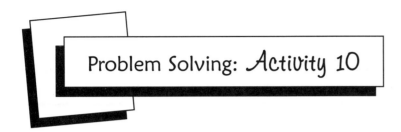

Problem Solving: Activity 10

Name _____

Listen to each situation. Then write your answers to the questions.

1. Martha and her friends wanted to see a new movie that was just released. When they got up to the ticket counter, the cashier said the movie was sold out for that showing. The girls decided to go to a different movie instead.

   What was the problem? _____

   How did the girls solve the problem? _____

   What else could they have done? _____

   _____

2. Blake's friends always borrowed money from him for lunch, but they never paid him back. Finally, Blake stopped bringing money to school so his friends couldn't borrow it from him anymore.

   What was the problem? _____

   How did Blake solve his problem? _____

   What else could he have done? _____

   _____

3. Connie's French class is taking a trip to France during the summer. Connie's parents said she can go if she raises half of the money herself. Connie decided to get a job at the neighborhood grocery store to earn the money for her trip.

   What was the problem? _____

   How did Connie solve her problem? _____

   What else could Connie have done to earn money? _____

   _____

Name _____

Listen to each problem I describe. Then look at the solutions. Mark an **X** beside the answer you think is the best solution to the problem. Tell why you think that.

1. Karla and some of her friends are having a picnic at a local park. When Karla gets to the park, she realizes she forgot to bring sunscreen. What should she do?

   _____ go buy some sunscreen

   _____ borrow sunscreen from a friend

   _____ don't bother to use sunscreen

2. Michael wants to go swimming with some friends, but he can't reach his parents to ask permission. What should he do?

   _____ leave his parents a note telling them that he went swimming

   _____ call his mom's cell phone and leave a message

   _____ stay home

3. Imagine you received an offer in the mail to join a CD club. You think it's a great deal. What should you do?

   _____ fill out the application to join and mail it in

   _____ throw the application away

   _____ ask your parents about the club

4. Your friend's dog keeps running away. What should your friend's family do?

   _____ get rid of the dog

   _____ put up a fence

   _____ put the dog on a leash

76

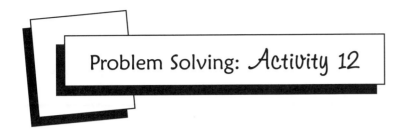

Name _____

Problems can often have more than one solution. Read each situation. Then answer the questions.

1. Imagine you have a cat. Your family is going on vacation and you'll be gone for a week.
   You can't take the cat with you. What is the problem? What are two things you could do
   to solve the problem?

   Problem: _____

   Solution #1: _____

   Solution #2: _____

2. Imagine your friends call and invite you to go to the water park with them. You want to go,
   but you don't swim very well. What is the problem? What are two things you could do to
   solve the problem?

   Problem: _____

   Solution #1: _____

   Solution #2: _____

3. Imagine you and your family planned to eat at your favorite restaurant. When you get to
   the restaurant, you see people waiting in line clear out the door. What is the problem?
   What are two things you could do to solve the problem?

   Problem: _____

   Solution #1: _____

   Solution #2: _____

4. Imagine you and your friend are 14 years old. Your stepdad agrees to drop you both off at the
   movies. When you get to the theater, you find out the movie you were going to see is rated R.
   What is the problem? What are two things you could do to solve the problem?

   Problem: _____

   Solution #1: _____

   Solution #2: _____

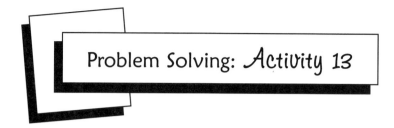

Problem Solving: *Activity 13*

Name _____

Listen to each situation and tell what you would do.

1. What would you do if you tore your new shirt?

2. What would you do if you hated your haircut?

3. What would you do if you needed help learning a new computer program?

4. What would you do if you heard one friend saying mean things about another friend of yours?

5. What would you do if you didn't get invited to a party that all of your friends are invited to?

6. What would you do if a project you were working on was taking more time than you expected?

7. What would you do if you missed the date to register for a class you wanted to take?

8. What would you do if you were invited to a party that you didn't want to go to?

9. What would you do if you were at a movie and the people around you kept talking?

10. What would you do if you fell, and after three days, your arm still hurt?

11. What would you do if you tried out for the lead in a school play and didn't get the part?

12. What would you do if you didn't agree with your friend about what to do on the weekend?

13. What would you do if someone you don't like keeps asking you to hang out?

14. What would you do if you wanted to start a new hobby?

15. What would you do if you saw some other students looking at you and laughing?

16. What would you do if you needed to find something at the bottom of a swimming pool, but couldn't open your eyes underwater?

17. What would you do if you wanted to look at something that was too small to see well?

18. What would you do if you found a package in the park and no one else was around?

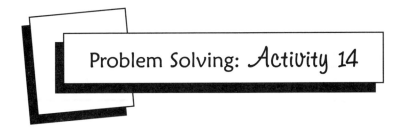

Name _____

Listen to each situation. Tell what problems each one could cause.

1. Some of your friends were swearing in front of your parents.

2. Karen had friends over to her house without her parents' permission.

3. You decide to go out with some people you don't know very well.

4. Your mom asked you to pick up your little sister at school and you forgot.

5. You left for school in a hurry and left your watch on your dresser.

6. The last person to leave the apartment forgot to close the windows.

7. One of the students in your math class is constantly tapping his pencil.

8. You share a room with your brother. You like to listen to music while you study, but your brother doesn't.

9. Your family is always in a hurry, so most of the time you eat fast-food meals for dinner.

10. You really hate going to the dentist, so you skip your appointment.

11. You make plans with two people for the same day.

12. You fix lunch and leave the food on the counter for several hours.

13. You take a phone message for your dad but forget to give it to him.

14. You are getting ready for work and find the water isn't working.

15. You have a date, but you don't know what time he's picking you up. You try to call the person, but you can't reach him.

16. You are trying to fix your bike, but the bolt is too tight for you to loosen.

17. You are helping your brother with a project when your friend calls to ask you to go to a movie.

18. You plan to talk to your algebra teacher after school because you have a test tomorrow and you need some extra help. You are scheduled to sell tickets for the school play after school.

79

Name _____

People use many things to help prevent problems from happening. Tell what problem each item below helps us prevent. Look at the pictures to help you with your answers.

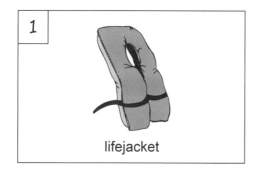

1. lifejacket

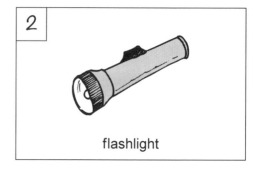

2. flashlight

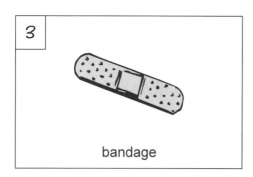

3. bandage

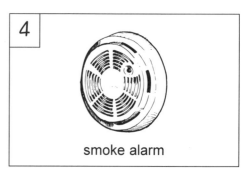

4. smoke alarm

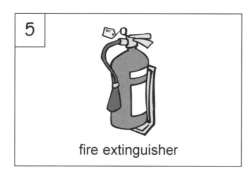

5. fire extinguisher

6. sugar free gum

7. stop sign

8. suntan lotion

100% Language—Intermediate

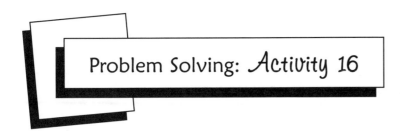

Problem Solving: Activity 16

Name _____

Like most kids your age, there are probably certain places you aren't allowed to go and certain things you aren't allowed to do. Most likely, there are reasons you have these rules. Read each item. Then write at least two reasons why you might not be allowed to go to the place or do the activity listed.

1. go to an R-rated movie

_____

_____

2. walk alone at night

_____

_____

3. go somewhere without telling your family

_____

_____

4. leave your home unlocked

_____

_____

5. chat on-line with someone you don't know

_____

_____

6. go boating

_____

_____

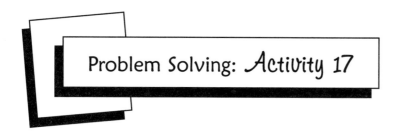

Name _____

We all need rules to help avoid certain problems. For example, people who drive must not go faster than the speed limit in order to avoid getting a ticket or causing an accident.

Read each rule. Then write a sentence telling one problem it helps prevent.

1. You must raise your hand to talk during a class discussion. _____

_____

2. Read the directions before beginning an assignment. _____

_____

3. Don't open the door to a stranger. _____

_____

4. Don't answer the phone if your parents aren't home. _____

_____

5. Keep your pet on a leash outdoors. _____

_____

6. No running in the halls. _____

_____

7. Call home if you're going to be late. _____

_____

8. You must be a certain height to ride some of the rides at an amusement park. _____

_____

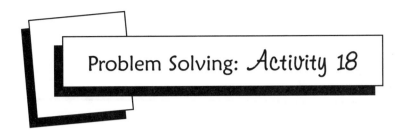

Problem Solving: *Activity 18*

Name _____

Read each situation. Then answer the questions.

1. A family pulls in to a campsite to camp. The campers have two small children and a dog. The only site available has a cliff nearby and there is a river below.

   What is one problem that could occur in this situation? _____

   _____

   What could be done to prevent this problem? _____

   _____

2. A group of boys are playing in an old lot. There is a large abandoned building that has been condemned. The windows are boarded shut and there is a **No Trespassing** sign on the building.

   What is one problem that could occur in this situation? _____

   _____

   What could be done to prevent this problem? _____

   _____

3. Mrs. Justice and her five-year-old daughter went shopping at the mall. It was a rainy day so the mall was very crowded.

   What is one problem that could occur in this situation? _____

   _____

   What could be done to prevent this problem? _____

   _____

Look at the following services and organizations. Work with a partner to discuss what kinds of problems they help solve.

24-hour customer service

Web-site addresses for businesses/stores

Save the Whales

AAA auto service

Educational HELP lines

Abuse Hotlines

American Cancer Society

GOODWILL

Toys for Tots

Save the Rain Forest

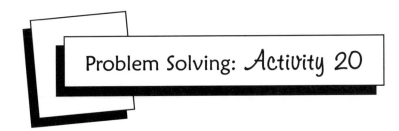

Name _____

It is important to plan ahead in order to avoid problems. Imagine you are planning the events below. Write two things you might do to plan each event. Then write one problem you would be avoiding by doing each thing.

Class Picnic

What I'd do: _____

_____

One problem this would prevent: _____

_____

Something else I'd do: _____

_____

One problem this would prevent: _____

_____

Surprise Party

What I'd do: _____

_____

One problem this would prevent: _____

_____

Something else I'd do: _____

_____

One problem this would prevent: _____

_____

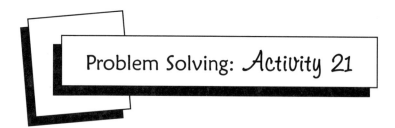

People solve many problems while on the job. Look at each job. Write at least two problems that each one helps solve or prevent.

1. **police officer**

_____

_____

2. **umpire**

_____

_____

3. **principal**

_____

_____

4. **chaperone**

_____

_____

5. **store security guard**

_____

_____

6. **lifeguard**

_____

_____

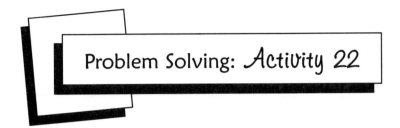

Name _____

Listen to each problem. Then tell one good solution and one bad solution to the problem. Why might someone choose each solution?

1. You're playing a game and you need one more player to have enough for two teams. As you're trying to decide what to do, a classmate walks by. He's nice, but not very popular, and he's not very good at sports.

2. You're walking down the sidewalk. You hear some kids across the street calling you names and making fun of you.

3. Your family is going to the park to listen to some bands perform. Your dad has packed a cooler with sandwiches and drinks. When you get there, you find you can't take coolers into the park.

4. While shopping, you find a cool necklace. Your mom doesn't think it's a good idea to spend the money on it because she says it isn't very well made and will break easily.

5. You go to a dance with your friends at a local teen club. Your friend's stepmom drops you off at home by curfew, but you realize you left your jacket at the club.

6. You live next door to an elderly woman. Your family realizes that you haven't seen the woman for a couple of days.

7. You are waiting for your mom to pick you up from school for an 11:00 dentist appointment. It's now 10:45 and your mom hasn't arrived yet.

8. You have to work with a partner on a science project that is due in two weeks. Your partner refuses to set a time to get together to work on the project.

9. You decided to get a job to earn money for a new stereo. You also enjoy playing sports. When you get your report card, you see your grades have dropped.

10. You finished your English report, but you haven't proofread it. You know you'll lose points if you turn it in late, but you'll also lose points for grammatical errors and spelling errors. The report is worth one-third of your grade.

87

Oftentimes, problems arise when we don't have enough information about something. An example of this is when we're looking at an advertisement and important details have been left out.

Look at the advertisement below. Find three pieces of information that have been omitted. To help you, think about what questions you would have if you were going to attend the concert.

Saturday, July 14, 7:00 p.m.

Concert to Benefit United Way!

Order Tickets in Advance
Closed on Sundays

What information is missing from this advertisement?

1. _____

2. _____

3. _____

Now look in a newspaper or magazine at an advertisement for an event in your area. If possible, cut it out and put it in the box below. Is there important information missing? Why is it important for advertisers to include so many details?

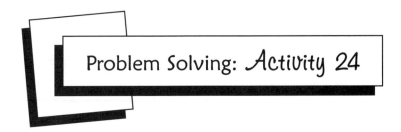

Problem Solving: *Activity 24*

Each of us has problems that we have to solve every day. Identify three problems you encountered during the day or that you saw happen to someone else. Write the problems and what you or the other person did to solve each one. Then tell another way each problem could have been solved.

Problem:
Solution:
Another Solution:
Problem:
Solution:
Another Solution:
Problem:
Solution:
Another Solution:

Dear Parent/Caregiver,

In class, we've been learning how to identify and solve problems in various kinds of situations. As your child develops this skill, his language skills will strengthen and he will be more successful in school and other social situations.

Following are some are some activities you can do to help your child become a better problem solver.

- When you see something wrong, talk about why it's a problem. Then ask your child to tell you what should be done. For example, if you see a child riding a bicycle in the street, ask your child to tell you what the problem is and what should be done.

- Make up problem situations and ask your child to solve them. Here are some ideas:

    - Your child wants to watch a special program on TV, but someone else is already watching her favorite show. What could he do?
    - Your child left his math book at school and can't do his assignment. What could he do?
    - Your child borrowed something from a friend and lost it. What could he do?
    - Your child broke a rule. What should be done?

- Talk about current events with your child. Ask him to identify the problem and tell what is being done to solve it. Then talk about other possible solutions.

- Discuss personal family problems as they arise. Again, talk about what the problem is and what could be done to solve it.

- Discuss why decisions are made in order to solve a problem. You can talk about simple examples, like why you might have to change a dinner menu when you learn there will be someone extra for dinner, to something more complex, like why you can't purchase something because you need to save money.

- Take time to talk about situations that occur at home, at school, and in the community. This will help your child make better decisions in all situations.

Thanks for helping your child learn!

Sincerely,

_____
Clinician

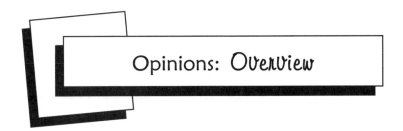

Opinions: Overview

People have opinions on just about everything, from relatively simple concepts like what musical group is better to more complex ideas such as world politics. Many times each day, we share our opinions as part of our day-to-day communications with others.

Unfortunately, students whose language skills are weak often have difficulty expressing their opinions. This may be one factor that contributes to the level of success these students have with conversational and written language skills. Older students may have an especially hard time if this skill is weak because they will tend to base decisions and actions on the opinions of others rather than taking time to formulate their own thoughts. The activities in this unit are based on common, everyday situations and are designed to give your students practice with the important language skill of expressing opinions.

■ Using the Activity Pages

- Before beginning the activities in this unit, talk about what opinions are. Explain that when you give an opinion there is no right or wrong answer.

- Review the vocabulary on each page. Teach any words that may be new to your students.

- Discuss things that might influence opinions, like personal experiences, likes and dislikes, what friends and family think, etc.

- Expand on the situations presented on the activity pages. Involve your students by asking them to share personal experiences that might be similar.

- On activity pages that have more complex situations, you may want to brainstorm information you already know about a topic. Then have your students determine what information is fact versus opinion.

- If your students are unfamiliar with the topics on the activity pages, have them use resource materials to find information in order to complete the activity.

- Talk about the words *agree* and *disagree*. These are introduced in later activities.

- Send the activity pages home for additional practice.

■ Expansion Activities

- If your students are ready, talk to them about the impact people's opinions can have on decisions that are made. Explain the idea of "the majority rules." Depending on the age and level of your

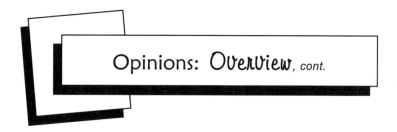

students, illustrate the concept by talking about things such as which TV program to watch or issues like who will be the next President. Introduce the concept that even though you have an opinion, things may not turn out the way you want them to.

• Provide opportunities for your students to give their opinions on class work. For example, give them two or more choices of a new story and ask for their opinions about which one the class should read. Remind them that the majority rules.

• Have your students make charts to show how people's opinions are different. For example, students could find out how many people have the same favorite color, flower, sport, or type of music.

• Expand the above activity by asking students to choose a product or restaurant they like. Ask them to take a poll to find out who else in the class likes the product and who doesn't, or who has never used the product. Then have them present information to try to convince their classmates that it's a good product and why they should use it. When they have finished, have them take their poll again. How many of their classmates changed their opinions? Discuss why it's okay to change your opinion based on new information.

Opinions: Progress Chart

Name _____

	Days / Trials			Comments
Activity 1				
Activity 2				
Activity 3				
Activity 4				
Activity 5				
Activity 6				
Activity 7				
Activity 8				
Activity 9				
Activity 10				
Activity 11				
Activity 12				
Activity 13				
Activity 14				
Activity 15				
Activity 16				
Activity 17				
Activity 18				
Activity 19				
Activity 20				
Activity 21				
Activity 22				
Activity 23				
Activity 24				

Opinions: *Activity 1*

Name _____

Look at the pictures. Circle the pictures that show activities you enjoy doing. Tell why you like each one.

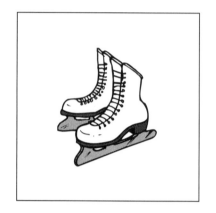

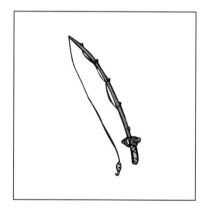

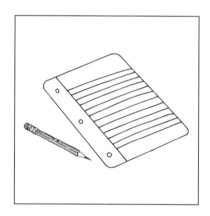

Name _____

Look at the pictures in each row. Circle the pictures of things you like and tell why you like them. Then mark an **X** on the pictures of things you don't like and tell why you don't like them.

1.

2.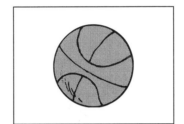

3.

4.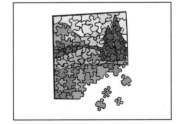

5.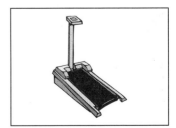

Opinions: *Activity 3*

Name _____

Listen to each question I ask. Then circle the picture that shows which thing you would rather do. Tell why.

1. Would you rather play football or go to a concert?

2. Would you rather watch a movie at home or at the theater?

3. Would you rather earn money mowing lawns or delivering newspapers?

4. Would you rather study for a test alone or with a study group?

Opinions: Activity 4

Name _____

Listen to each question I ask. Then mark an **X** on the picture that shows which thing you would rather do. Tell why.

1. Which means of transportation would you rather use when taking a trip?

2. If you had your choice, would you rather get up early in the morning or sleep in?

3. Would you rather have friends over for pizza or go on a picnic?

4. On a rainy day, would you rather play a board game or read a good book?

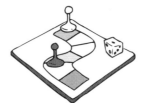 

5. Imagine you're helping your friend run for class president. Would you rather give a speech to convince others to vote for her or make campaign posters?

Name _____

Look at the pictures. I'm going to tell you about them. Then answer my questions.

1. Olivia takes music lessons every Saturday morning. This Saturday Olivia isn't feeling well. Do you think she should be allowed to miss her music lesson? Why?

2. Matt has a science test tomorrow. While he's studying, a friend calls and invites him to come over and watch a movie. Should Matt be allowed to go? Why?

3. Tracy belongs to a club that meets only once a month. This month the meeting is scheduled for the same night that she has soccer practice. She doesn't want to miss practice because then she won't get to start the next game. Should Tracy be allowed to miss her club meeting? Why?

4. Brian is going to receive a lower grade in math than he thought because the teacher said he hadn't turned in three assignments. Should Brian be allowed to make up the assignments?

98

Opinions: Activity 6

Name _____

Listen to my questions and tell me what you think.

1. Would you rather eat broccoli or carrots? Why?

2. Would you rather eat pizza or a hamburger? Why?

3. Would you rather read a mystery or a science fiction book? Why?

4. Would you rather drink Pepsi or Coke? Why?

5. Would you rather run or ride a bike for exercise? Why?

6. Would you rather watch a comedy or a horror film? Why?

7. Would you rather call a friend or e-mail one? Why?

8. Would you rather play *Trivial Pursuit* or *Monopoly*? Why?

9. Would you rather work at a grocery store or a fast-food restaurant? Why?

10. Would you rather write a book report or take a test? Why?

11. Would you rather pierce your ears or your eyebrow? Why?

12. Would you rather go to a football game or a concert? Why?

13. Would you rather collect rocks or stamps? Why?

14. Would you rather decorate for the holidays or leave things as they are? Why?

15. Would you rather visit an aquarium or the Empire State Building? Why?

16. Would you rather wear contacts or glasses? Why?

17. Would you rather be a photographer for a magazine or for a portrait studio? Why?

18. Would you rather help create an animated movie or a movie with real people? Why?

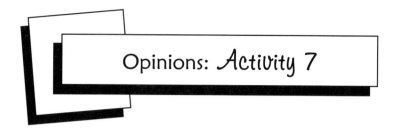

Opinions: Activity 7

Name _____

Listen to my questions and tell me what you think.

1. Would you rather vacation at the beach or go sightseeing in a big city? Why?

2. Would you rather watch a movie on video or DVD? Why?

3. Would you rather stay at a hotel with an indoor swimming pool or one with an outdoor pool? Why?

4. Would you rather go to small shops or a large mall to buy what you need? Why?

5. Would you rather buy your friend a book or a CD for a gift? Why?

6. Would you rather walk in the park or along the beach? Why?

7. Would you rather have a hamster or a snake for a pet? Why?

8. Would you rather have a salad or French fries with your lunch? Why?

9. Would you rather help your neighbor paint a fence or plant flowers? Why?

10. Would you rather visit Canada or Mexico? Why?

11. Would you rather learn French or Japanese? Why?

12. Would you rather act in a play or help with the stage sets? Why?

13. Would you rather write an article for the school newspaper or take photographs for the paper? Why?

14. Would you rather take a pottery class or a photography class? Why?

15. Would you rather study a unit on weather or animal habitats? Why?

16. Would you rather learn to scuba drive or skydive? Why?

17. Would you rather judge an art contest or a writing contest? Why?

18. Would you rather plant a vegetable garden or a flower garden? Why?

Opinions: Activity 8

Name _____

Understanding the difference between fact and opinion will help you make decisions more easily. A fact is something you can prove. An opinion is what you think about something. Not everyone has the same opinion. Look at the example.

FACT: *Coffee is made from coffee beans.*   **OPINION:** *Coffee tastes good.*

Now listen as I read some statements. Decide whether each one is a fact or an opinion. Then circle the correct answer.

1. A cruise would be a fun vacation.   Fact   Opinion

2. Twins should always dress the same.   Fact   Opinion

3. Chickens lay eggs.   Fact   Opinion

4. Baby lions are called *cubs*.   Fact   Opinion

5. Traveling is the best way to find out about new places.   Fact   Opinion

6. Germs can make people sick.   Fact   Opinion

7. Magic tricks are easy to learn.   Fact   Opinion

8. The President of the United States does a good job.   Fact   Opinion

9. The TV show *Wheel of Fortune* is a great show.   Fact   Opinion

10. Earth is a planet.   Fact   Opinion

Opinions: Activity 9

Name _____

Listen to what I say. Then circle whether it is a fact or an opinion.

1. Wearing baggy pants is cool.   Fact   Opinion

2. Smoking is bad for your health.   Fact   Opinion

3. Clowns are funny.   Fact   Opinion

4. It's scary to walk outside at night without a flashlight.   Fact   Opinion

5. The Olympic Games are exciting to watch.   Fact   Opinion

6. Fishing should be banned.   Fact   Opinion

7. All people should be vegetarians.   Fact   Opinion

8. People should be allowed to take photos during concerts.   Fact   Opinion

9. There are four quarts in a gallon.   Fact   Opinion

10. A barometer measures air pressure.   Fact   Opinion

11. A microscope makes small things look bigger.   Fact   Opinion.

12. Science projects are interesting.   Fact   Opinion

Name _____

Listen to what I say. Then circle whether it is a fact or an opinion. If it is an opinion, tell whether you agree or disagree and why.

1. An ostrich is a large bird that can run very fast, but cannot fly.   Fact   Opinion

2. Onions taste awful.   Fact   Opinion

3. A roller coaster is fun to ride.   Fact   Opinion

4. A rattlesnake is poisonous.   Fact   Opinion

5. Radar uses radio waves to spot objects.   Fact   Opinion

6. Playing baseball is boring.   Fact   Opinion

7. A laughing hyena is ugly.   Fact   Opinion

8. A mummy is a dead body that has been preserved.   Fact   Opinion

9. A quarter is worth twenty-five cents.   Fact   Opinion

10. Learning to ice-skate is easy.   Fact   Opinion

11. Spiders have eight legs and spin webs.   Fact   Opinion

12. Tennis shoes are more comfortable to wear than sandals.   Fact   Opinion

Opinions: *Activity 11*

Name _____

Look at each picture. Then write one fact and one opinion about each picture.

1.   Fact: _____

   Opinion: _____

2.   Fact: _____

   Opinion: _____

3.   Fact: _____

   Opinion: _____

4.   Fact: _____

   Opinion: _____

5.   Fact: _____

   Opinion: _____

6.   Fact: _____

   Opinion: _____

7.   Fact: _____

   Opinion: _____

8.   Fact: _____

   Opinion: _____

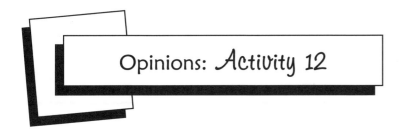

Name _____

Listen to each situation. Then tell me what you think.

1. Imagine you're at a coffee shop having lunch with some friends. When the server brings your check, you notice that she hasn't charged you for one of your drinks. One of your friends thinks you should just pay what's on the check and not tell the server she made a mistake. What do you think? Why?

2. You find out a kid in your class has a crush on you, but you don't like him. Your best friend thinks you should just tell him you don't like him. What do you think? Why?

3. Imagine you get in trouble at school and your parents ground you. You don't think what you did is a big deal, but you know you shouldn't have done it. Do you think you should have been grounded? Why?

4. Your friend hurt his back lifting heavy boxes at work. He asks you what he should do. What would you tell him? Why?

5. Mr. Fillmore found out his daughter and her best friend were angry with each other. Should Mr. Fillmore talk to his daughter about the situation or let her deal with it on her own? Why?

6. Some in-line skaters wear knee pads, elbow pads, and helmets. Do you think wearing all of those accessories is necessary? Why?

7. Chase heard a rumor about one of his friends that he knew wasn't true. What do you think Chase should do? Why?

8. Imagine you had a huge argument with one of your best friends and your feelings were really hurt. Another friend told you to just forget about it because it's over. What do you think? Why?

9. Jason's family is going to a family reunion over the holiday weekend. Jason's friends are having a big party the same weekend and they're upset because Jason chose to go to the reunion. Do you think Jason made a good decision? Why?

10. Stacy's family recently moved to this area, and her parents are concerned because Stacy hasn't made many new friends yet. Stacy doesn't really want to join any of the clubs or teams at school, but her parents encourage her to join anyway. Do you agree with Stacy's parents? Why?

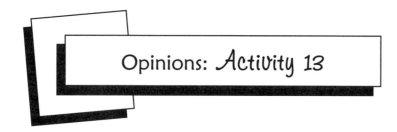

Name _____

Listen to each situation. Then tell me what you think.

1. Beth's youth group volunteers at a local soup kitchen once a month. Do you think this is a good project for a youth group? Why?

2. Imagine you have a friend whose parents never ask him to check in with them. Do you think that's a good idea? Why?

3. Mrs. Cross is the third-grade teacher. She rewards her students with stickers when they bring their homework back on time. The fourth-grade teacher, Mrs. Gill, doesn't think it's necessary to give her students rewards for bringing their homework back because that's what they're supposed to do. Do you think you should be rewarded for something you're supposed to do? Why?

4. Tracy asked her parents if she could have five dollars a week allowance for washing the dishes every day. Tracy thought this was a good way to save some money to buy something she wanted. Tracy's mom agrees, but Tracy's dad doesn't believe in giving an allowance to children. Who do you agree with? Why?

5. Carl's parents said he can't have his own bike until he's ten years old because that's when his brother got his first bike. Do you think that's fair to Carl? Why?

6. Zach is supposed to run in a race to raise money for a special organization. When he wakes up, he's feeling sick. He decides to run the race anyway. Do you think Zach made a good decision? Why?

7. Mrs. Thomas is cleaning her garage. She decides to throw away everything she doesn't use anymore, even if it's not broken. Do you agree with Mrs. Thomas's decision regarding her unused items? Why?

8. Mr. Finney refused to buy candy from the children who came to his door. He thought the children would just waste the money they made. Do you think Mr. Finney understood why the children were selling candy? Why?

9. Jeff was not behaving very nicely. His mom scolded him for his behavior in front of his friends. Do you think Jeff's mom did the right thing? Why?

10. Todd's parents have the same rules for Todd that they have for his younger brother. Todd is four years older than his brother. Do you agree that the rules should be the same for both boys? Why?

106

Listen to each situation and answer my questions.

1. The school cafeteria serves the same lunch two days a week. They think this saves them money. Do you think this is a good idea, or do you think there should be more variety even if it costs more? Why?

2. Tom needs money to buy a stereo. He has a baseball card collection his uncle gave him a few years ago. He wants to sell the collection to help make the money he needs, but his parents don't want him to. Do you think selling his collection is a good idea? Why?

3. Kristin's mom only allows her to watch TV for one hour a day during the week. Sometimes Kristin doesn't have homework and gets bored. She doesn't see anything wrong with watching more than one hour of TV. Do you think Kristin should be allowed to watch more TV? Why?

4. Denny wants a TV for his room. He hasn't saved enough money to buy a new one, but his neighbor is selling a small TV at a garage sale. Denny isn't sure it's a good idea to buy a used TV. What do you think? Why?

5. Paula doesn't like to run or lift weights, so for exercise she does water aerobics. Some of her friends make fun of her because they think she's not really getting much exercise. What do you think? Why?

6. Some schools have a program that allows students to do community service for credit. Do you think that would be a good program to have at your school? Why?

7. Terry's family is going to move right before his senior year in high school, and he's upset. His aunt said he could live with her in order to finish school with his friends. If he does, he won't see his family much until he graduates. Terry's parents don't think it's a good idea. Do you agree with them? Why?

8. Kelsey was sick and missed taking a final chapter test at school. She asked if she could make up the test, but her teacher said she would have to take a zero. Do you agree with the teacher's decision? Why?

9. Imagine that your school encourages all students who take Spanish to join Spanish Club. The policy is that if you participate in the club, you will receive extra credit points for the class. Some students don't want to join Spanish Club. Do you think the policy is fair? Why?

10. Mr. Dexter's geography students must complete a research paper. They must include specific pieces of information that Mr. Dexter said they can find easily on the Internet. Greg is in this class, but he doesn't own a computer. He explained this to his teacher and asked for extra time to complete the assignment. Mr. Dexter told Greg that his grade would be lowered if his paper wasn't turned in on time. Do you think Mr. Dexter was fair to Greg? Why?

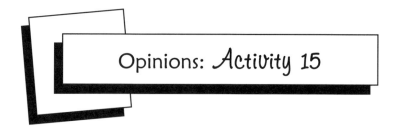

Opinions: Activity 15

Name _____

Listen and answer my questions.

1. Imagine you were going to visit relatives in a large city. They talked about taking you to the opera. Would you want to go? Why?

2. What is the best movie you've ever seen? Why?

3. What kind of car do you think is the coolest car ever made? Why?

4. Is it important to wear the latest clothing styles? Why?

5. What do you think is the most important subject in school? Why?

6. Do you think sports or music is more important to offer in school? Why?

7. Which type of music do you think is better, country or rock? Why?

8. Some schools ban books that they think are inappropriate for students to read. Do you think schools should be allowed to ban books? Why?

9. Imagine your school doesn't allow students to wear shirts with writing on them. Do you agree with this rule? Why?

10. Who do you think is the most popular musical group? Why?

11. If you could interview anyone in the world, who would it be? Why?

12. Jim is having trouble reading. His parents want him to get a tutor. Do you think getting a tutor is a good idea? Why?

13. Angela's family is having friends over for dinner. Her parents told her she had to stay home all evening to play with their friends' small children. Do you think it's fair that Angela has to stay home? Why?

14. Bill's parents want to buy his grandmother a computer so she can communicate with family and friends more easily and more often. His grandmother thinks it's too much money to spend. Do you agree with Bill's parents or with his grandmother? Why?

15. Telemarketers call at all hours during the day and evening to sell their products. Do you think they should be prevented from making these sales calls? Why?

Brainstorm some things you know about each action. Then use your ideas to write one fact and one opinion about each one. Finally, share your opinions with someone else. Find out if that person agrees with you or not.

1. Some things I know about using a computer for research:

_____

_____

_____

Fact: _____

Opinion: _____

2. Some things I know about taking care of animals:

_____

_____

_____

Fact: _____

Opinion: _____

3. Some things I know about playing ice hockey:

_____

_____

_____

Fact: _____

Opinion: _____

Opinions: Activity 17

Name _____

Read each situation. Mark an **X** on the answer that best matches your opinion. Then tell why you think so.

1. Karen is supposed to be saving money for a school trip. One afternoon a group of her friends invite her to the mall to go shopping. In your opinion, what should Karen do? Why?

    _____ Karen should stay home.

    _____ Karen should go to the mall, but she should set a limit on how much money she can spend.

    _____ Karen should go to the mall, but she shouldn't spend any money there.

2. You've heard the saying, "Honesty is the best policy." Do you think that's true all the time, though? Imagine you overheard someone say something about a friend of yours that would hurt your friend's feelings. In your opinion, what should you do if your friend asks you about what you heard? Why?

    _____ I would lie to my friend about what I heard.

    _____ I would tell my friend even though it would hurt her feelings.

    _____ I wouldn't tell my friend anything.

    _____ I would tell a teacher what I heard so she could tell my friend.

3. Imagine your brother is in sixth grade. He wants to play baseball and join Art Club. Both baseball practice and Art Club meetings are held after school. When you're in sixth grade, it's okay to miss some practices, but not when you're in seventh or eighth grade. In your opinion, what should your brother do? Why?

    _____ He should only get involved in one of the activities now.

    _____ He should participate in both activities now and then choose which activity he likes better after sixth grade.

    _____ He should find out if next year it would be okay to miss Art Club meetings for practice.

4. Jason is a friend of yours, but sometimes he is very bossy. The other kids are upset with Jason and they're beginning to avoid him. In your opinion, what would be the best thing you could do to help the situation? Why?

    _____ I would talk to Jason about how he acts.

    _____ I would tell the other kids to accept Jason just the way he is.

    _____ I would stop being Jason's friend.

Opinions: *Activity 18*

Name _____

People have different opinions about many things. Read each question. Then write two or three sentences stating your opinion and why you think that.

1. Should there be year-round school?

_____

_____

_____

2. Should teachers give homework on weekends?

_____

_____

_____

3. Should there be a city curfew on weeknights? If yes, what time should it be?

_____

_____

_____

4. Should there be a city curfew on weekends? If yes, what time should it be?

_____

_____

_____

5. Should teachers give students detentions when they're late to class three times?

_____

_____

_____

Read each fund-raising situation. In your opinion, is each effort worthwhile? Write your answer on the lines. Be sure to include the reasons for what you think.

Selling candy to raise money for school activities

_____

_____

_____

_____

Holding events like races and bowling tournaments to raise money for cancer research

_____

_____

_____

_____

Raising $1,000,000 to build a fountain in front of a new hospital

_____

_____

_____

_____

Holding a benefit dance (The admission charge is $3.00 or three canned goods. Proceeds will go to the local food pantry.)

_____

_____

_____

_____

Name _____

Read each question. Then write your opinion on the lines. Be sure to include the reasons for what you think.

1. Are zoos good places for animals? Why?

    _____

    _____

    _____

    _____

    _____

2. Should the space program continue? Why?

    _____

    _____

    _____

    _____

    _____

3. Should companies be required to spend money to keep rivers and oceans clean? Why?

    _____

    _____

    _____

    _____

    _____

Read each question. Then write your opinion on the lines. Be sure to include the reasons for what you think.

1. Should people be required to recycle? Why?

_____

_____

_____

_____

_____

_____

_____

2. Do you think chemicals that may cause diseases should be used to spray for insects? Why?

_____

_____

_____

_____

_____

_____

_____

Opinions: Activity 22

Name _____

Choose one of the topics from Activity 20 or 21, or think of another issue that interests you, and write it on the line. Then write a short description of what your opinion about this topic is.

Issue/Question: _____

My Opinion: _____

_____

_____

Next take a poll to see what other people think about this issue. Write each person's name in the chart. Put a checkmark in the correct column to tell whether the person agrees or disagrees with your opinion. Ask the person to give you reasons for her opinion.

Name	Agree	Disagree	Why
_____	_____	_____	_____
_____	_____	_____	_____
_____	_____	_____	_____
_____	_____	_____	_____
_____	_____	_____	_____
_____	_____	_____	_____
_____	_____	_____	_____
_____	_____	_____	_____

Now that you've heard some other people's opinions, do you think the same as you did before or have you changed your mind?

Advertisers use both facts and opinions to try to get us to buy their products. Look at the advertisement below. Circle the information in the ad that is based on opinions.

Now look in a newspaper or magazine for an advertisement. Cut it out and put it in the box. Then circle the opinions. Do you agree with what the advertisement says?

Name _____

We have opinions about things that happen every day. Use the chart below to describe situations when you have an opinion. A situation might include things like a movie you see, what you have for dinner, or what time you should go to bed. Write your opinion about the situation, and include information about other people's opinions. What facts did you base your opinions on?

Situation:

My opinion:

Parent:	Friend:	Other: _____
☐ Agree ☐ Disagree	☐ Agree ☐ Disagree	☐ Agree ☐ Disagree

Facts:

· ·

Situation:

My opinion:

Parent:	Friend:	Other: _____
☐ Agree ☐ Disagree	☐ Agree ☐ Disagree	☐ Agree ☐ Disagree

Facts:

· ·

Situation:

My opinion:

Parent:	Friend:	Other: _____
☐ Agree ☐ Disagree	☐ Agree ☐ Disagree	☐ Agree ☐ Disagree

Facts:

· ·

Situation:

My opinion:

Parent:	Friend:	Other: _____
☐ Agree ☐ Disagree	☐ Agree ☐ Disagree	☐ Agree ☐ Disagree

Facts:

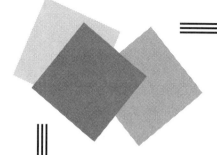

Dear Parent/Caregiver,

In class, we've been learning about expressing opinions. We've also talked about the fact that people have different opinions about things. It's important for your child to know how to express her opinion in a way that is clear to other people.

Here are some ways you can help your child practice expressing opinions.

- When making family decisions, sit down together and discuss various options. Have everyone give his or her opinion. Then vote on what to do. For example, you might want to decide what curfew should be on weekends, where you should go on vacation, or which movie to watch as a family.

- When family members have different ideas on what should be done, have each member write her thoughts on a sheet of paper. Next read the ideas aloud without telling who wrote each one. Then have everyone vote on which idea they agree with most.

- Talk about everyday issues, comparing your opinions. You might talk about family gatherings, a recent movie you've seen, current fashions, local news events, or even politics.

- Read an editorial from the newspaper together. Talk about whether you agree or disagree with the writer's point of view.

Understanding others' opinions and the ability to express her own opinions will help your child become a better reader, writer, and communicator.

Thanks for helping your child learn!

Sincerely,

_____

Clinician

Inferencing: Overview

Inferencing is the ability to use one's prior knowledge and apply it to new information we see, hear, or read in order to deduce something. It is a skill we use daily, often without even being aware of it. Unfortunately, some students don't develop this skill on their own. As a result, they may experience difficulties in areas such as question comprehension, reading comprehension, identifying details, understanding important information, and justifying their opinions. The activities in this unit are designed to give students an opportunity to practice making inferences using examples from real situations your students may encounter. Practicing this important language skill will help them become better communicators.

■ Using the Activity Pages

- Before beginning the activities in this unit, talk about what it means to make inferences and why it's important.

- Review the vocabulary on each page. Teach any words that may be new to your students.

- As your students work through the activities, the inferences they make will become more complex. Talk about the connection between making inferences and making predictions.

- Send the activity pages home for additional practice.

■ Expansion Activities

- Help your students continue to practice making inferences. Take time during the week to discuss situations when your students have made inferences. You may reuse Activity 24 on page 145 for this purpose.

- Before beginning a class activity, show your students the materials they'll be using. Ask your students to tell you what they think the activity is going to be and how they know.

- Before beginning a new story, ask your students to infer what the story is about based on the book's title or cover art only. As you read the story, stop periodically and ask your students to make inferences or predictions about why something happened or what will happen next based on what they know. Later, have students talk about whether their inferences were correct.

- As your students become more skilled at making inferences, talk about the fact that a person's inference about someone or something may or may not be correct. For example, if a classmate came to school and was unusually quiet, you might think she didn't feel well. After talking to her, you find out that what actually happened is that her pet died. Ask your students to tell about things they've inferred on a day-to-day basis and whether their inferences were right or wrong. You may reuse Activity 24 on page 145 for this activity.

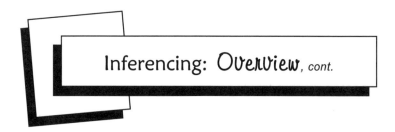

- Write brand names of items on index cards. Name the items one at a time and have your students tell what they think the product is and what it's used for. You may also have your students bring in names of items they see that convey meaning. Have them share the item names with the class. Does everyone agree with what the item is for?

- Have your students work with a partner to invent a product and give it a name. Then have each pair of students tell the name of their product and see if the other students can guess what it is.

- Bring in a variety of newspapers. Have your students choose articles and make inferences from the headlines. Then have them read the articles to determine if they were correct. You may reuse the bottom of Activity 24 on page 145 for this activity.

- Do role-play activities to help your students infer emotions from body language. Write emotion words like *angry*, *happy*, and *surprised* on index cards. Give one to each student. Have the student show through body language only what emotion is on his card. Ask the other students to guess what emotion the student is showing.

Inferencing: Progress Chart

Name _____

	Days / Trials			Comments
Activity 1				
Activity 2				
Activity 3				
Activity 4				
Activity 5				
Activity 6				
Activity 7				
Activity 8				
Activity 9				
Activity 10				
Activity 11				
Activity 12				
Activity 13				
Activity 14				
Activity 15				
Activity 16				
Activity 17				
Activity 18				
Activity 19				
Activity 20				
Activity 21				
Activity 22				
Activity 23				
Activity 24				

Inferencing: *Activity 1*

Name _____

Listen and then follow my directions.

1. Lunches are over for the day. Circle the picture that shows how you know.

2. The principal is not happy about what he's hearing. Circle the picture that shows how you know.

3. The girl burned her hand while baking cookies. Circle the picture that shows how you know.

Listen and then follow my directions.

1. Mark an **X** on the picture that makes you think someone is in high school. Tell why you think so.

2. Mark an **X** on the picture that makes you think that winter is coming. Tell why you think so.

3. Mark an **X** on the picture that makes you think someone is hurt. Tell why you think so.

Listen and then follow my directions.

1. Danny didn't want to go to the store with his mom. Point to the picture that shows how you know.

2. Todd was surprised at the information in the letter. Point to the picture that shows how you know.

3. Alex had a hard time getting up in the morning. Point to the picture that shows how you know.

 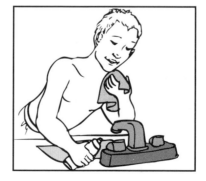 

People often make inferences based on what they see. Look at the pictures below. What do you know about the person who has these things? Tell how you know.

1

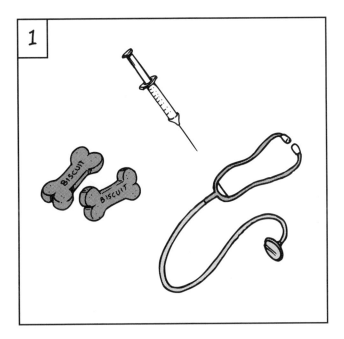

2

3

4

Inferencing: Activity 5

Name _____

Look at the pictures and then answer my questions.

1. What kind of pet do you think the person has? How do you know?

2. What kind of message did the man receive? How do you know?

3. What kind of food is the woman eating? How do you know?

4. What kind of movie is the girl watching? How do you know?

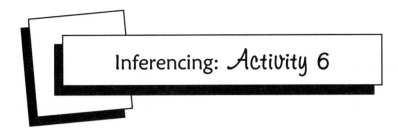

Name _____

Our knowledge of what things look like or are used for helps us identify objects.   Listen to the clues I give you and tell me what I'm describing.

1. I am a musical instrument.
    I come with sticks.
    You hit me.
    What am I?

2. I can be white or brown.
    I break easily.
    I come from chickens.
    What am I?

3. I have pockets and zippers.
    I hold books and papers.
    Students carry me to school.
    What am I?

4. I'm made of paper.
    You write addresses on me.
    People use me to send items to others.
    What am I?

5. I'm made of metal.
    I have two wheels.
    People ride me.
    What am I?

6. I'm a vehicle.
    I have emergency medical equipment.
    I'm used to transport people to the hospital.
    What am I?

7. I live in a jungle.
    I'm very large.
    I have big ears and a trunk.
    What am I?

8. I move slowly on land.
    I can swim in the water.
    I carry my house with me everywhere I go.
    What am I?

9. I have a trunk.
    I can be different sizes and colors.
    People drive me.
    What am I?

10. I have keys.
     I have a memory.
     I have a monitor.
     What am I?

11. I have many seats.
     I have many cars.
     I move very fast.
     What am I?

12. I have several pages.
     I have articles and advertisements.
     Some people receive me every day.
     What am I?

127

Inferencing: *Activity 7*

You can identify places by what you know about them. Read the descriptions below and identify each place.

1. I hold lots of water. Sometimes I'm made of cement. Kids like to splash in me. _____

2. I'm very large. I have many rooms. Kings and queens live here. _____

3. I cover a large area. Wild animals live here. I have a thick growth of trees. _____

4. I have a lot of dirt. I can be in a large, open area or in someone's backyard. Flowers and vegetables grow in me. _____

5. Many people come here every day. They come here before and after trips. They bring their luggage with them when they come. _____

6. I'm usually oval in shape. I have several lanes. Cars move very fast on me. _____

7. I'm in New York Harbor. I was a gift from France. My full name is Liberty Enlightening the World. I hold a torch. _____

8. I'm in South Dakota. I'm found on the side of a mountain. I have four faces. _____

Now think of two other places. Write clues that describe each place. Then ask a classmate to identify the place you described. Did the person guess correctly?

9. _____

_____

10. _____

_____

Inferencing: Activity 8

Name _____

The tools a person uses can tell us what that person does for a living. Read each list below. Tell me what job you think the person who uses these tools has.

1

mop

bucket

dustcloths

vacuum

rags

cleaners

2

stethoscope

syringes

scale

bandages

thermometer

cotton swabs

Medical Tendencies of Infants

3

tool belt

hammer

nails

drill

level

saw

wood

4

bench

gavel

black robe

courtroom

documents

5

computer

telephone

filing cabinet

intercom

letter opener

6

hoist

oil

rags

tires

air pump

tire gauge

antifreeze

Inferencing: Activity 9

People often make inferences based only on what they hear. Listen and then answer my questions. For each item, mark an **X** on the line next to the answer(s) you think are correct.

1. Imagine you're in the lunchroom and you hear a noise behind you. What do you think the person behind you might be eating for lunch? Tell why you think that.

   _____ pudding   _____ carrots

2. Imagine you're talking on the phone to a friend and you hear water running. What might your friend be doing? Tell why you think that.

   _____ taking a shower   _____ washing dishes

3. Imagine you're home alone. You think your mom has to work until 5:00 p.m. At 4:00 p.m., you hear the garage door open. What do you think is happening? Tell why you think that.

   _____ your mom got off work early   _____ someone is breaking into your garage

4. Imagine that every time you walk by the school office you hear someone coughing and sneezing. Who do you think is sick? Tell why you think that.

   _____ the secretary   _____ your teacher

5. Imagine you're walking down the street on July 5th. You hear a high-pitched whirring noise and then a loud bang. What do you think caused the noise? Tell why you think that.

   _____ someone set off a firecracker   _____ someone's car backfired

6. Imagine you're in your garage and you hear screeching tires and then a loud noise. What do you think just happened? Tell why you think that.

   _____ a car accident   _____ someone got a flat tire

7. Imagine you're outside and you hear sirens. What would you think? Tell why you think that.

   _____ a building is on fire   _____ someone is hurt   _____ a race is about to begin

8. Imagine you're walking in a park and you hear screaming. What would you think? Tell why you think that.

   _____ someone is hurt   _____ children are playing   _____ someone dropped a picnic basket full of food

We often make guesses about someone or something based on what we see happening. Listen to the situations I describe and answer my questions.

1. Imagine you're at a restaurant. You see the woman at the next booth looking at her watch and then toward the door over and over again. What would you think?

2. Pretend you're talking to your friend Marla after school. She's in a hurry to leave because she has a softball game. The next day when you see Marla, she's limping. What would you think?

3. When you come back to school after winter break, the girl who sat beside you isn't there. What would you think?

4. Imagine you're at the grocery store and you see a woman and her daughter filling the cart with bags of snacks and hot dog and hamburger buns. What would you think?

5. When you go outside, you see several cars parked at your neighbor's house. You don't recognize most of them. Why do you think those cars might be there?

6. Imagine you're driving down the highway and see large pieces of rubber on the road. What do you think happened?

7. When you come out of school, you see tire marks on the street in front of the school. What do you think happened?

8. Imagine you're walking toward the grocery store and you see broken glass in front of the store. What might have happened?

9. You're going to your friend's house for dinner. When you arrive, the house is dark and no one answers the door. What might have happened?

10. When you get home from school, you see water all over the driveway, but nowhere else. What might have happened?

11. When you walk by the detention hall at school, you see your best friend sitting with another student at one of the tables. What would you think?

12. Imagine your bus goes by the high school each day on your way to school. In the fall, you see students with musical instruments lined up on the grass outside. What would you think?

Inferencing: Activity 11

Name _____

We often infer things from what we see or from what someone tells us. Listen to the situations I describe and then answer my questions.

1. Jessica said that her brother's room looked like a tornado had hit. What do you think her brother's room looked like?

2. Kent's mom found a pair of pants shoved in the corner of Kent's closet. When she told Kent about them, she said they looked like they could stand up on their own. Why do you think Kent's mom said that?

3. Sarah's friends called and wanted her to go out with them. Sarah said she couldn't because she was a wreck. What do you think Sarah meant?

4. The Johnsons decided to stop and visit their cousins. As they drove up to the house Mr. Johnson said, "Hey, I don't think anyone's home." Why do you think Mr. Johnson would say that?

5. When Debbie came downstairs, her little brother giggled and said, "I bet Debbie has a date." Why do you think Debbie's brother thought that?

6. After seeing the look on his dad's face, Jason called his friend and told him he'd better wait to ask his parents about going to the concert. What kind of mood do you think Jason's dad was in?

7. Mrs. Jensen said, "From the look of things on the bridge, I think we're going to be late." What do you know about the traffic on the bridge?

8. Travis went inside to call his uncle. When he came back outside, Travis said he thought his uncle must have gone away for the weekend. Why do you think Travis said that?

9. Kris asked Paula to go to the library with her. Paula said, "Gee, I don't know, I have a lot to do. I have errands to run and laundry to finish." Do you think Paula wanted to go the library?

10. Diana bought a raffle ticket from her neighbor. Later, Diana said, "This must be my lucky day." Why do you think Diana thought it was her lucky day?

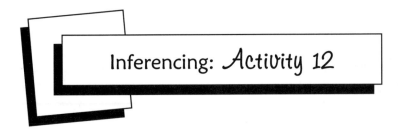

Inferencing: *Activity 12*

Name _____

Read each situation. What would you infer?

1. How would you know from talking to someone that the person was from a foreign country, even if he didn't tell you?

2. If you walked into someone's home, how could you tell the person has a new baby?

3. How could you tell if your brother is in a bad mood?

4. How would you know if a motorcycle drove by?

5. What might you see that would tell you there had been a bad storm?

6. How could you tell that someone is grilling in his backyard?

7. What would you hear that would make you think someone has a swimming pool?

8. What would you think if you saw someone pull into a gas station, and then saw the person leave without getting gas?

9. What would make you think that your friend's sister likes to read?

10. What would you think if you came home and your parents were playing cards by candlelight and your brother was reading using a flashlight?

11. What would you hear to make you think that you were near a fairground?

12. Without being told, what would make you think that you should take your shoes off before going into someone's home?

13. If you were selling candy door-to-door, what might make you think you shouldn't go to a particular place?

14. What would you think if you saw a group of kids picking up trash in a local park?

15. What would you think if you saw someone searching through a dumpster?

100% Language—Intermediate   133

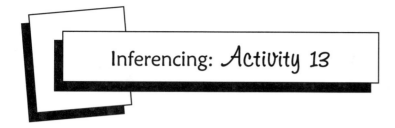

Inferencing: *Activity 13*

Name _____

Read each item and infer what the person means. Circle the letter of the answer you think is correct.

1. I slept like a baby.
    a. The person slept well.
    b. The person slept poorly.

2. I really shouldn't eat that.
    a. The person doesn't like the food.
    b. The person has an allergy to the food.

3. Are you kidding? I'm not going to touch that spider!
    a. The person can't reach the spider.
    b. The person is afraid of the spider.

4. If I ride a roller coaster, I can't open my eyes!
    a. The person hates to ride roller coasters.
    b. Roller coasters hurt the person's eyes.

5. Yuck! What did you do, put the whole salt shaker in this soup?
    a. The soup tastes great.
    b. The soup tastes too salty.

6. I'm afraid we're going to have to walk if we don't see a gas station soon.
    a. The person thinks it's a nice night for a walk.
    b. The person thinks they will run out of gas if they don't get some soon.

7. I wish I had a nickel for every time they played that song!
    a. The person wants to make money.
    b. The song has been played several times.

8. I'll be hard pressed to find a date at this point.
    a. The person thinks it will be difficult to find a date in such a short time.
    b. The person has plenty of time to find a date.

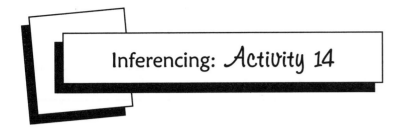

Making inferences is easy when you think about the facts you know. Listen and answer my questions. Think about what you know about each kind of situation before you answer.

1. How would you know if your friend had allergies?

2. How can you tell if someone is in a hurry?

3. If you were introduced to someone you'd never met before, why might you think he owned a dog?

4. Imagine there's a light breeze blowing. What would you know if you saw a cup blow off of the picnic table?

5. How would you know which team the person sitting beside you was cheering for?

6. What would you think if you heard someone say, "Oh my gosh!"

7. What would you think if you heard someone say, "I feel like an idiot!"

8. What would you think the temperature is where your cousin lives if he said, "It's like a sauna outside"?

9. How do you think your mom feels if she says, "Boy, what a rat race!"

10. What did the coach mean when he yelled, "Let's get 'em back now!"

11. How would you know if someone was sick just by looking at the person?

12. Imagine someone who is usually very talkative is sitting quietly at her desk when you walk into the classroom. What would you think?

13. Imagine you saw a large crowd gathered at a park. Each person there was holding a candle. What would you think?

14. What would you think if you heard someone say, "I'm not eating in there again"?

15. What would you think if you heard someone say, "Not on your life!"

Inferencing: Activity 15

Sometimes when we listen, we need to use what we see, what we hear, and the facts that we know to infer what the speaker wants us to do. Read each situation. Then write what you think the speaker wants the other person to do.

1. Jason's dad was working in the yard. He looked at Jason and said, "Boy, it's hot out here. I could sure use something to drink." What does Jason's dad want him to do?

   _____

2. Maria's mom looked out the window and said, "The grass is really looking shaggy." What does Maria's mom want her to do?

   _____

3. Mr. Jones came downstairs. When he saw the mess in the kitchen, he said, "Steve, come on, it's time to leave. Let's get this show on the road." What does Mr. Jones want Steve to do before they leave?

   _____

4. Kim's mom has a rule that all of Kim's things must be picked up before she goes to bed. Kim was reading a book when she heard her mother say, "Kim, hurry up! Quit wasting time!" What does Kim's mom want her to do?

   _____

5. John is talking to his girlfriend on the phone. He hears his dad say, "John, we're leaving in five minutes." What does John's dad want him to do?

   _____

6. Terry is in his room reading a book when he hears his mom say, "This would be a lot easier if I didn't have to do it alone." What does Terry's mom want him to do?

   _____

We often picture people in our minds based on what we hear about them. Listen to the following descriptions. Then write two or three sentences to tell what you think each person would be like. The first one is done for you.

1. Tim eats like a bird.

   Tim doesn't eat very much. Tim is a picky eater. Tim is thin.

2. Martha was like a bull in a china shop.

   _____

   _____

3. Monty's arms were as big as tree trunks.

   _____

   _____

4. When Philip had his mind made up he was like a runaway train.

   _____

   _____

5. Gracie was like a ray of sunshine.

   _____

   _____

6. Morgan's eyes are always bigger than her stomach.

   _____

   _____

7. Andrew is always the last one to leave.

   _____

   _____

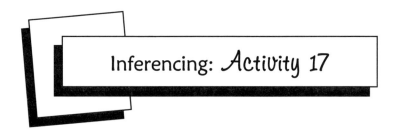
When you listen to sports results, you really have to pay attention to know which team won. Read each sports announcement. Then write which team won and which team lost each game.

1. *The Bulldogs raced past the Greyhounds.*

   WON _____   LOST _____

2. *The Spartans drop their fourth in a row to the Knights.*

   WON _____   LOST _____

3. *The Giants trample the Miners 21 to 12.*

   WON _____   LOST _____

4. *The Tigers fell to the Rangers in overtime.*

   WON _____   LOST _____

5. *Iowa checks Wisconsin in double overtime.*

   WON _____   LOST _____

6. *The Hawks were toppled by the Ravens 2 to 1.*

   WON _____   LOST _____

7. *The Lakers remain undefeated following Saturday's game with the Twisters.*

   WON _____   LOST _____

8. *The Groundhogs dig their way to the top over the Rattlers in the first playoff game.*

   WON _____   LOST _____

Inferencing: Activity 18

Name _____

Sports announcers use colorful language to describe events. You have to pay attention in order to know what happened. Read each statement that an announcer might say. Then write what you think the announcer is talking about.

1. Let's get ready for the sports wrap-up!

   _____

2. Para's solo shot was deposited into the seats.

   _____

3. Roland finally connects with the ball.

   _____

4. Tonight the Vikings and the Bears hook up.

   _____

5. The Blue's pitcher is having a rough game. They're really hitting him tonight.

   _____

6. If Ryan gets on base, he's a sure run because he's got a good set of wheels!

   _____

7. The Mavericks keep the Spirit off the board!

   _____

8. I think Zimmerman's corner kick clinched the championship for the Racers.

   _____

9. That putt bought Miller a place in the playoff round.

   _____

10. The Cubs and the Cardinals split a pair.

   _____

A company's name can give you an idea of what kind of business it is. Look at the signs. What does the name tell you about each company?

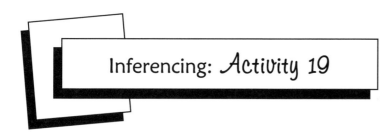

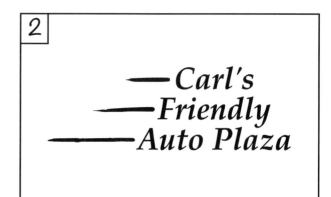

Inferencing: Activity 20

Name _____

The name of a product often tells you something about the product. Look at each name below. What does it tell you about each product? What would the product be used for? Write your answers on the lines. Then compare your answers to your classmates'.

1. **Miracle Wash**

_____

_____

2. **Crud Cutter**

_____

_____

3. **La-Z-Boy**

_____

_____

4. **Goo-Be-Gone**

_____

_____

5. **Battery Booster**

_____

_____

6. **Head & Shoulders**

_____

_____

Name _____

Companies use advertising to try to influence you into buying their products. TV commercials are one type of advertising. People who make commercials use certain techniques to try to get you to think something specific about products.

Read the techniques below. What do you think advertisers want you to believe when they use these techniques? Do you think these types of TV commercials are effective? Write your answers on the lines. Then compare your answers to your classmates'. Do you all agree?

1. racecar driver to sell cars _____

_____

2. teenagers laughing and having fun to sell soda _____

_____

3. thin people to sell clothing _____

_____

4. young women to sell cosmetics _____

_____

5. famous people to sell products _____

_____

6. action activities to sell vitamins _____

_____

7. sports stars to sell sports equipment, like athletic shoes _____

_____

8. tropical locations to boost airline sales _____

_____

Inferencing: *Activity 22*

Name _____

Newspaper headlines tell you at a glance what an article is about. Look at the headlines. What do you think the article for each headline is about? Write your answers on the lines. Then compare your answers to your classmates'. Did you agree?

1. **Eastern States Wake to Blanket of Snow**

   _____

2. **Budget Cuts Hit Schools Hard**

   _____

3. **Camping Chaos Overnight**

   _____

4. **Strong Storms Pound Area**

   _____

5. **Teen Awakened by Fire Fighters**

   _____

6. **FARMERS FEAR FLOODING**

   _____

7. **TOP GRADS**

   _____

8. *Mother Nature Not Very Motherly*

   _____

9. **Clowning Around**

   _____

10. **FIGHTING FLAB**

   _____

Look at the advertisement and then answer the questions.

1. Why did the owners of the mall think they needed to put up this sign?

   _____

   _____

2. What deals do the merchants want you to think you'll receive if you shop there?

   _____

3. Why do the store owners think that offering bigger discounts than normal is a good idea during the remodeling?

   _____

   _____

4. Why do you think the mall owners want you to know that reconstruction isn't a problem?

   _____

   _____

Inferencing: Activity 24

Name _____

Use this page to keep track of situations during the day when you make inferences. Share your situations with the class. At the bottom of the page, comment on a newspaper headline or a book title you've seen. What inference did you make when you read it? Share your ideas with the class.

Situation: _____

What inference did I make? _____

_____

Was my inference correct? _____

_____

Situation: _____

What inference did I make? _____

_____

Was my inference correct? _____

_____

Situation: _____

What inference did I make? _____

_____

Was my inference correct? _____

_____

Headline/Book Title: _____

What inference did I make? _____

_____

After reading, was my inference correct? _____

_____

Dear Parent/Caregiver,

In class, we've been learning to make inferences. In order to make good inferences, it's necessary to think about what you already know. Then you have to figure out what else you know from what you see, hear, or read. As we get older, we are expected to know what is going on around us and why. These expectations are present in school, in the community, and at home. Following are some ideas you can do at home with your child to help improve his ability to make inferences.

• When shopping, point out items that are unfamiliar to your child. Ask him to figure out what each item is or what it's used for.

• When watching TV or a movie, turn off the sound and ask your child to tell you what he thinks the people are saying or doing. Or at the commercial break, talk about what you think will happen next in the show based on what you already know.

• Ask your child about everyday things and how he knows certain information. You might include simple things, like the fact you know someone had something to eat because there are dishes in the sink, to more complex things like knowing something serious has happened when there is an interruption in TV programming for an "important newsbreak."

• Talk about common inferences you make every day, like expecting certain kinds of things to happen in a movie based on the type of music you hear or reading a person's body language and knowing he's happy, sad, or angry.

• Ask your child to tell you about a book he's reading for school. Before he finishes the story, ask him to tell what he thinks will happen next based on what he knows. Have him tell you when he finishes the story if he was right.

By practicing this skill with your child, you'll help him learn to look at what he knows and make good inferences.

Thanks for helping your child learn!

Sincerely,

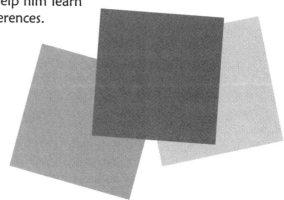

_____

Clinician

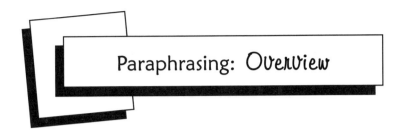

Paraphrasing: Overview

Paraphrasing is restating something in your own words. It is different from summarizing in that you do not necessarily shorten the information. Paraphrasing is an important skill your students need when writing reports, explaining information, or repeating directions. Good paraphrasing skills also contribute to better reading comprehension because the reader is able to reword the information mentally and retain it better.

The activities in this unit include functional, real-life situations. The lessons will teach your students how to paraphrase, beginning with the basic skill of using synonyms and progressing in difficulty through tasks requiring more practical applications of paraphrasing.

As your students improve their ability to paraphrase, they will be better able to follow conversations and understand information presented to them. They will also become more confident in their reading and writing skills.

■ Using the Activity Pages

- Before beginning the activities in this unit, talk about what paraphrasing is and when and why we use the skill. Explain how it is different from summarizing.

- Review the vocabulary on each page. Teach any words that may be new to your students.

- You may choose to present the pages verbally rather than requiring your students to give written responses.

- Have your students use a dictionary or thesaurus as necessary to complete the activity pages.

- Send the activity pages home for additional practice.

- Use Activity 23 on page 172 and Activity 24 on page 173 to introduce the skill of summarizing.

■ Expansion Activities

- Throughout the day, have your students restate directions in their own words.

- Read short stories aloud. Then have your students rewrite them in their own words.

- Give your students messages to pass along to someone else, like the principal or another teacher. Check to see if they relayed the message correctly.

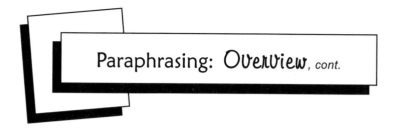

- Have your students read newspaper articles about current events and then share in their own words what has happened.

- Have your students research various topics and write or give oral reports about what they've learned.

- Talk about what figurative language is and why people use it. Make a list of common figurative language phrases and have your students reword them. Then have your students make a list of sayings they hear throughout the day in school, on television, or just when they're out and about. Talk about what these sayings mean.

- For fun, tell your students sayings used when you were younger. Have them tell you the sayings kids use today that mean the same thing.

Paraphrasing: Progress Chart

Name _____

	Days / Trials			Comments
Activity 1				
Activity 2				
Activity 3				
Activity 4				
Activity 5				
Activity 6				
Activity 7				
Activity 8				
Activity 9				
Activity 10				
Activity 11				
Activity 12				
Activity 13				
Activity 14				
Activity 15				
Activity 16				
Activity 17				
Activity 18				
Activity 19				
Activity 20				
Activity 21				
Activity 22				
Activity 23				
Activity 24				

Paraphrasing: Activity 1

Name _____

Synonyms are words that mean the same thing or almost the same thing. Use the words in the word box to write a synonym for each bold word. (*Hint: You won't use all of the words in the word box.*)

1. **insect**   _____

2. **stair**   _____

3. **soil**   _____

4. **road**   _____

5. **restaurant**   _____

6. **custodian**   _____

7. **friend**   _____

8. **cap**   _____

9. **cook**   _____

10. **carpet**   _____

11. **student**   _____

12. **doctor**   _____

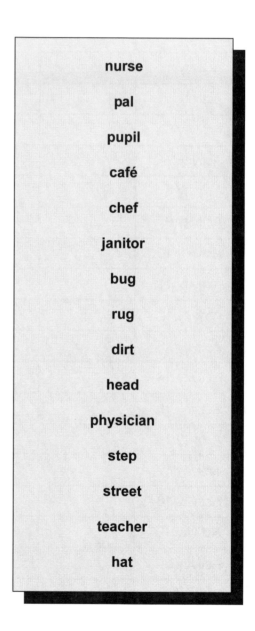

nurse

pal

pupil

café

chef

janitor

bug

rug

dirt

head

physician

step

street

teacher

hat

Name _____

Write a synonym, or word that means the same thing, next to each bold word.

1. **big** _____

2. **shut** _____

3. **small** _____

4. **thin** _____

5. **damp** _____

6. **stir** _____

7. **mad** _____

8. **late** _____

9. **soda** _____

10. **snooze** _____

11. **ill** _____

12. **speak** _____

13. **noisy** _____

14. **joyful** _____

15. **finish** _____

16. **snapshot** _____

17. **enjoyable** _____

18. **leap** _____

19. **circular** _____

20. **display** _____

When we paraphrase, we substitute one word or phrase for another without changing the meaning. Read each sentence. Circle the letter next to the word that means almost the same thing as each bold word.

1. The ancient **dwelling** was intriguing.

   a. house   b. office

2. The children were **delighted** when the piñata finally broke open.

   a. disgusted   b. pleased

3. Carol was disappointed when she found the **error** on her paper.

   a. mistake   b. answer

4. Billy's new shoes were **filthy** when he came home from the field trip.

   a. dirty   b. torn

5. Perry **tossed** the things he found in the attic into a large box.

   a. kept   b. threw

6. Jackie hoped to have a chance to **sketch** the landscape while on vacation.

   a. draw   b. photograph

7. Richard was studying to be an **attorney**.

   a. accountant   b. lawyer

8. The eclipse of the moon **fascinated** the children.

   a. amazed   b. bored

When we paraphrase, we substitute one word or phrase for another without changing the meaning. Read each sentence. Circle the letter next to the word that means almost the same thing as each bold word.

1. Quinn was eager to **complete** the project.

   a. finish   b. start

2. The group was just about finished with their **rehearsal**.

   a. work   b. practice

3. Jessie had trouble making friends because he was so **bashful**.

   a. shy   b. outgoing

4. Mrs. Carter wanted to insure the package because it was **fragile**.

   a. harmful   b. breakable

5. The store had a sale on **shears**.

   a. scissors   b. knives

6. The nurse **discovered** the mistake on the patient's chart.

   a. found   b. created

7. The mechanic needed to **examine** the engine.

   a. finish   b. inspect

8. Charlie needs to write a check to pay his **dues**.

   a. fees   b. refund

Paraphrasing: Activity 5

Name _____

When you paraphrase, sometimes you can use one word to replace multiple words in a sentence and still keep the same meaning. Read each sentence. Then look in the word box to find one word that could replace each bold phrase. Write the word on the line next to the sentence. (*Hint: You won't use all of the words in the word box.*)

jewelry	currency	shapes	transportation
sciences	planets	trees	writing utensils
furniture	tools	appliances	relatives

1. Bob enjoyed visiting his **aunts, uncles, and cousins** over spring break. _____

2. When he moved, Jack bought a new **couch, coffee table, and chairs** for his living room. _____

3. Kyle liked his job selling **dishwashers, stoves, freezers, and refrigerators**. _____

4. Mrs. Jessop went to the hardware store to buy **a saw, a hammer, and a screwdriver**. _____

5. Carlie was pleased when her grandmother gave her a special **necklace and bracelet**. _____

6. Juan is fascinated by **botany and zoology**. _____

7. The Kramers planted several **maples, oaks, and pines** on their property. _____

8. Mr. Collins bought several new **pencils and pens** before starting his new teaching job. _____

9. Charles relies on public **buses or the subway** to get to work. _____

10. Sheila took all the **quarters and two-dollar bills** she'd saved to the bank. _____

Paraphrasing: *Activity 6*

Name _____

When you paraphrase, sometimes you can use one word to replace multiple words in a sentence and still keep the same meaning. Read each sentence. Then look in the word box to find one word that could replace each bold phrase. Write the word on the line next to the sentence. (*Hint: You won't use all of the words in the word box.*)

finish	hibernate	expensive	decrease
dissolve	calculate	increase	improve
island	diagram	ancestors	migrated

1. Patti needed to buy a new winter coat, but she didn't want something **very costly**. _____

2. **Thoroughly mix** the powder in milk to make instant pudding. _____

3. Jason and his dad watched as the ducks **flew south** for the winter. _____

4. We didn't see many bears on our trip because they had already begun to **sleep for the winter**. _____

5. Steve needed to **draw a picture of** the go-cart he wanted to build. _____

6. Jessica wanted to **cut down on** the amount of salt she put in the recipe. _____

7. Clay decided to **add to** the number of sit-ups he did every morning. _____

8. Will was ready to **wrap up** his last report for the year. _____

9. Jersey was eager to research her **family's relatives**. _____

10. The crew found themselves stranded on the **land surrounded by water**. _____

Name _____

When you paraphrase, sometimes you can change more than one word in a phrase and still keep the same meaning. Look at each bold phrase. Choose a phrase from the box that means the same thing and write it on the short line. Then write a sentence using the new phrase. The first one is done for you.

1. **beautiful woman** _pretty lady_

   There is a pretty lady on the cover of that magazine.

2. **tiny pebble** _____

   _____

3. **thick woods** _____

   _____

4. **large ship** _____

   _____

5. **quick kids** _____

   _____

6. **fancy car** _____

   _____

7. **torn coat** _____

   _____

8. **wise teacher** _____

   _____

9. **humorous show** _____

   _____

10. **center seat** _____

    _____

funny movie

ripped jacket

~~**pretty lady**~~

huge boat

dense forest

middle chair

fast children

smart instructor

small rock

luxury auto

156

Paraphrasing: Activity 8

Name _____

When you paraphrase, sometimes you can change more than one word in a phrase and still keep the same meaning. Look at each bold phrase. Choose a phrase from the box that means the same thing and write it on the short line. Then write a sentence using the new phrase.

1. **roam the woods** _____

   _____

2. **gory movie** _____

   _____

3. **detest insects** _____

   _____

4. **vacant lot** _____

   _____

5. **perfect getaway** _____

   _____

6. **multiple ideas** _____

   _____

7. **famous author** _____

   _____

8. **short statement** _____

   _____

9. **latest developments** _____

   _____

10. **nasty odor** _____

    _____

scary show
most recent events
wander the forest
many thoughts
hate bugs
great escape
well-known writer
empty space
brief remark
bad scent

Paraphrasing: *Activity 9*

Replace one word from each phrase with a word from the word box. Write the new phrase on the short line. Then write a sentence using the new phrase. The first one is done for you. (*Hint: You won't use all of the words in the word box.*)

1. **recall the number**   <u>remember the number</u>

   <u>Do you remember the number of kids on the team last year?</u>

2. **tiresome group of people** _____

   _____

3. **tastes terrible** _____

   _____

4. **several pages** _____

   _____

5. **annual event** _____

   _____

6. **spare tire** _____

   _____

7. **horse was a champion** _____

   _____

8. **successful lawyer** _____

   _____

9. **courageous soldier** _____

   _____

10. **beneath the surface** _____

    _____

winner
~~remember~~
awful
scent
many
boring
under
yearly
lucky
extra
attorney
brave

Paraphrasing: *Activity 10*

Name _____

Read the sentences and answer the questions. Circle the correct response.

1. If the team felt defeated, was it doing well?   Yes   No

2. If a person is guilty, is he innocent?   Yes   No

3. If a vase is modern, is it considered an antique?   Yes   No

4. If a person is inquisitive, does she ask a lot of questions?   Yes   No

5. If a person is thoughtless, does he care a great deal about things?   Yes   No

6. If people are puzzled about something, do they understand?   Yes   No

7. If a person is described as enchanting, is she well-liked?   Yes   No

8. If a child is gentle with animals, does he treat them roughly?   Yes   No

9. If a hole is massive, is it very large?   Yes   No

10. If you have numerous chores, do you have many chores to do?   Yes   No

11. If a hill is steep, is it hard to climb?   Yes   No

12. If the water is shallow, is it deep enough to dive?   Yes   No

13. If the woman's voice is melodic, is it easy to listen to?   Yes   No

14. If the food is tasteless, is it flavorful?   Yes   No

15. If a person is unaware of activity next to him, does he know what's going on?   Yes   No

16. If the cake is moist, is it dry?   Yes   No

17. If the twins are identical, do they look alike?   Yes   No

18. If two objects collide, do they hit each other?   Yes   No

Complete each sentence with a word or phrase that means the same thing as the bold word.

1. If Jeff is usually **punctual**, he is usually _____.

2. If Kelsey's bracelet is **fragile**, it _____.

3. If the storm made the children **frantic**, the children were _____.

4. If the bug Cheryl found was too **tiny** to pick up, the bug was _____.

5. If Franklin was **exhausted** from working out, he felt _____.

6. If a person got a ticket for **speeding**, she was _____.

7. If the rabbit sat **motionless** in the yard, the rabbit sat _____.

8. If the mask looked **grotesque**, it looked _____.

9. If the movie was **hilarious**, it was _____.

10. If the new museum piece was **ancient**, it was _____.

11. If Jason watches a movie and cleans his room **simultaneously**, he _____

    _____.

12. If Rita is **enthusiastic** about going on the picnic, she is _____.

13. If Clayton is **mischievous**, he is _____.

14. If a task is **complicated**, it is _____.

160

Name _____

Sometimes you can paraphrase information by replacing some of the words with words that mean the opposite. Read each sentence. Write an antonym for each bold word on the short lines. Then rewrite the sentence using the new words. Be sure the meaning of the sentence stays the same. The first one is done for you.

1. He couldn't carve the turkey because the knife **wasn't sharp**. _____was_____ _____dull_____

   <u>He couldn't carve the turkey because the knife was dull.</u> _____

2. Mrs. Sellers repainted the stripes because they **weren't straight**. _____ _____

   _____

3. The Crawford's **didn't accept** the package from the UPS driver. _____ _____

   _____

4. Corrine challenged the teacher about her test grade because she knew her answer **wasn't wrong**. _____ _____

   _____

   _____

5. Chris was surprised when she heard the news because she knew the report **wasn't true**. _____ _____

   _____

   _____

6. Carson recognized the man on the front page of the newspaper. He knew the man **wasn't guilty** of the crime. _____ _____

   _____

   _____

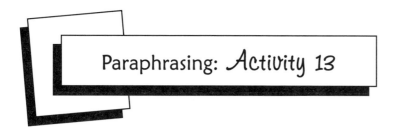

Name _____

Read each passage. Rewrite each one using synonyms for the bold words. Use a dictionary if you need help.

1. **Most** reptiles are land animals. However, many groups of reptiles can also **exist** in the water.

   _____

   _____

2. The cheetah is a **fascinating** mammal. This **beautiful** animal is a daytime hunter. The cheetah is very **swift**, running at speeds up to 70 mph.

   _____

   _____

3. Did you know a chameleon is **especially** well-suited to **residing** in bushes and trees? Its body is **broad**, giving it **stability** when climbing.

   _____

   _____

4. Lizards are interesting creatures. **Most** lizards **produce** eggs with leathery shells. Lizards are **rarely** attentive to their eggs once they are laid.

   _____

   _____

5. Garrett and Nathan **really like** going to the zoo with their **grandparents and cousins**. They **enjoy** watching the **huge** elephants **perform** tricks. They always **race** to the monkey house.

   _____

   _____

   _____

Paraphrasing: *Activity 14*

Name _____

Read each sentence. Rewrite it in your own words, changing as many words as possible but keeping the meaning the same. Then compare your sentences with your classmates' sentences.

1. Terrence was up late because he needed to finish his assignments.

   _____

2. Mr. Porter purchased a vehicle that was just like the man's next door.

   _____

3. Tonya was envious of Elizabeth because her family just got a new puppy.

   _____

4. The view was anything but ordinary.

   _____

5. Felix dropped the lid to the ketchup bottle and spent thirty minutes searching for it.

   _____

6. Clayton was eligible to play because he was still considered an amateur at the sport.

   _____

7. Monica was excited because she'd saved enough money to buy her mom's favorite cologne as a birthday gift.

   _____

   _____

8. Celeste was frustrated because the storage container she bought to put under the bed was so large it wouldn't fit.

   _____

   _____

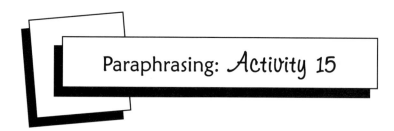
Read each sentence. Rewrite it in your own words, changing as many words as possible but keeping the meaning the same. Then compare your sentences with your classmates' sentences.

1. The huge ship had been submerged for one hundred years.

    _____

2. Emily couldn't remember all the digits in her friend's new phone number.

    _____

3. The lawyer was bound by his pledge to protect his client.

    _____

4. The cavern hadn't been explored for two decades.

    _____

5. The reporter indicated that the victim refused to comment on the attack.

    _____

6. The employees were requesting that everyone receive equal time off.

    _____

7. The chart made it easy to determine which class was ahead in the fund-raising contest.

    _____

    _____

8. The teacher told the students to estimate how long they thought the project would take.

    _____

    _____

Paraphrasing: *Activity 16*

Name _____

Work with a partner. First read each newspaper headline and talk about what you think each one means. Then use synonyms to reword each headline, making sure the meaning doesn't change. When you've finished, compare your answers to other groups' answers. Were they the same?

1. **5th Annual Rodeo Event Kicks Off Saturday**

   _____

2. **Chilling Temps Predicted**

   _____

3. **Soaring Fuel Prices Predicted**

   _____

4. **Technology Assists Company Growth**

   _____

5. **Leaders Seek Public Opinions**

   _____

6. **Researchers Believe Extraterrestrial Life Possible**

   _____

7. **Man's Best Friend Rescues Toddler**

   _____

8. *3-D Zooms Ahead*

   _____

Paraphrasing: *Activity 17*

Name _____

People often use figurative language to express their thoughts. Read each sentence. Then rewrite it in your own words, making sure the meaning stays the same. The first one is done for you.

1. I'd give my eyeteeth to hear that group again.

   I'd really like to hear that group again. _____

2. I need your advice like I need a hole in the head.

   _____

3. Marcie was afraid she'd fall flat on her face when she tried out for the play.

   _____

4. Allen didn't mean to step on anyone's toes when he changed the plan.

   _____

5. Most students thought the test was hard, but Tiana thought it was a piece of cake.

   _____

6. Elijah's parents were fit to be tied when he wasn't home by 10:00 p.m.

   _____

7. Chelsey smiled because she knew she pulled a fast one on her brother.

   _____

8. Jay knew that finding enough extra costumes for the play by next Friday was easier said than done.

   _____

   _____

Read each sentence. Write a sentence that tells another way to say each thing. Then compare your answers with your classmates' answers. The first one is done for you.

1. Toni said she was sorry to call at such a crazy hour.

    Toni apologized for calling so late/early. _____

2. I'm absolutely beat. I'm going home and crash.

    _____

3. Go ahead, you know the drill.

    _____

4. With the river on the rise, volunteers worked around the clock filling sandbags.

    _____

5. The team is all fired up!

    _____

6. The police were concerned because names were leaked to the press.

    _____

7. My mom flipped out when she heard what happened after the game.

    _____

8. Chuck found himself taking the heat for someone else's actions.

    _____

9. It's a delicate situation. We really have to thread the needle on this one.

    _____

10. Sherrie was worried that the volunteers would bail and she'd be on her own at the Hunger Drive.

    _____

Paraphrasing: *Activity 19*

Name _____

Speakers often use figurative language to express themselves. Read each bold phrase. Then reword it and use it in a sentence of your own. The first one is done for you

1. **pay an arm and a leg** *very expensive*

   Sheila knew it would be very expensive to get her car fixed after the accident.

2. **get up on the wrong side of the bed** _____

   _____

3. **clean as a whistle** _____

   _____

4. **clear as mud** _____

   _____

5. **get under my skin** _____

   _____

6. **could get ugly** _____

   _____

7. **bored to tears** _____

   _____

8. **get your act together** _____

   _____

Martin Luther King, Jr., and Helen Keller are two people who achieved great things during their lives. Below are statements that describe them. Paraphrase the information and use it to write a paragraph about each person.

→ **Martin Luther King, Jr. (1929-1968)**

- a clergyman
- a dynamic speaker
- a universally-known, black leader
- believed in and fought for civil rights and equality
- was jailed many times because of his mission
- believed in a nonviolent approach
- was awarded the Nobel Peace Prize in 1964
- assassinated on April 4, 1968

_____

_____

_____

_____

_____

→ **Helen Keller (1880-1968)**

- an amazing woman
- was blind and deaf from a fever at 19 months old
- was often angry as a child and threw temper tantrums, kicked and screamed, until worn out
- at age six, was examined by Dr. Alexander Graham Bell
- Anne Sullivan became her tutor
- Miss Sullivan taught her to read, write, and speak
- became well-known for her achievements in spite of severe disabilities
- spent later life working to improve conditions for people with disabilities

_____

_____

_____

_____

_____

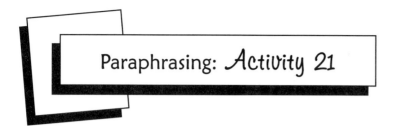
Read the following quotes. Then rewrite each one in your own words.

1. "The future belongs to those who believe in the beauty of their dreams." Eleanor Roosevelt

   _____

2. "Imagination is more important than knowledge." Albert Einstein

   _____

3. "Conscience is the inner voice that warns us somebody may be looking." Henry Louis Mencken

   _____

4. "It is often easier to fight for one's principles than to live up to them." Adlai Stevenson

   _____

5. "Be the change you wish to see in the world." Gandhi

   _____

6. "Happiness makes up in height for what it lacks in length." Robert Frost

   _____

7. "Everything is funny as long as it is happening to someone else." Will Rogers

   _____

8. "Booing like braying portrays true character!" Anonymous

   _____

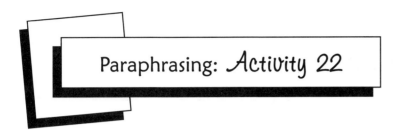

Name _____

Read the following quotes. Then rewrite each one in your own words.

1. "Happiness is not having what you want, but wanting what you have." Robbie H. Schachtel

_____

2. "A man is not old until regrets take the place of dreams." John Barrymore

_____

3. "Goodwill is the mightiest practical force in the universe." Charles F. Dale

_____

4. "The purpose of life is a life of purpose." Robert Byrne

_____

5. "A positive anything is better than a negative nothing." Anonymous

_____

6. "Let us never negotiate out of fear, but let us never fear to negotiate." John Fitzgerald Kennedy

_____

7. "Your success and happiness lie in you . . .. Resolve to keep happy, and your joy and you shall form an invincible host against difficulties." Helen Keller

_____

_____

8. "When you make a mistake, don't look back at it long. Take the reason of the thing into your mind, and then look forward. Mistakes are lessons of wisdom. The past cannot be changed. The future is yet in your power." Phyllis Battome

_____

_____

Look at this advertisement for a new brand of athletic shoes. Change at least five words in the original ad to make your own ad for these shoes.

PEAK Performance Shoes

Top 5 Reasons you can reach your PEAK with PEAK Performance shoes:

1. Athletic shoes you want and need at bargain prices
2. Styles for men, women, and children
3. Cool for Back-to-School!
4. Lightweight and Durable
5. Available at stores nationwide

GET YOURS TODAY!

PEAK Performance Shoes

Top 5 Reasons you can reach your PEAK with PEAK Performance shoes:

1.

2.

3.

4.

5.

Tell why the words you used in your advertisement will make people want to buy these shoes.

_____

_____

Name _____

Here's an opportunity to paraphrase information you come across during your day.

Write two directions you heard during the day at school, home, or work. Then reword the directions.

1. **Direction:** _____

   Reword: _____

2. **Direction:** _____

   Reword: _____

Now read a short newspaper or magazine article. Underline any words you could change and still keep the meaning of the information the same. Use the space below to rewrite the article in your own words.

_____

_____

_____

_____

_____

_____

_____

_____

_____

_____

_____

Dear Parent/Caregiver,

We've been practicing paraphrasing information, or restating something in your own words. This is an important skill that will help your child be a better communicator, both in conversation and in writing. Knowing how to paraphrase will be especially helpful to your child when she writes reports or research papers at school.

Here are some activities you can do with your child to help her practice paraphrasing.

• Ask your child to tell you about what she learned at school. You might ask her to explain how to do a particular type of math problem or what she learned in social studies that day.

• Have your child repeat directions you've given her in her own words.

• When you make a rule regarding a particular situation, have your child explain the rule and the consequences for breaking the rule in her own words. This will help both of you know she understands.

• Have your child read a paragraph from a textbook, magazine, or newspaper and then tell you what she read using her own words.

Thanks for helping your child learn!

Sincerely,

_____

Clinician

Answer Key

Suggested answers have been provided for most of the items; however, accept any reasonable responses.

■ ■ ■ Sequencing

page 10

1.

2.

3.

4.

page 11
1. girl with a ponytail
2. student sitting in last seat on bus
3. ketchup bottle
4. second base

page 12
1.

2. white, black
3. $19.00, $21.00
4.

page 13
1. minnow bucket, tackle box
2. Circle the towel.
3. Student will point to the appropriate rows.
4. Circle the woman.
   Mark an **X** on the girl.

page 14
1. feather, leaf, rock
2. elephant, lion, goat
3. second, minute, hour, day, month, year
4. rocket, train, motorcycle, bicycle
5. puddle, pond, lake, ocean
6. radio, telephone, television, satellite

page 15
2, 1
4, 3

page 16
4, 2
5, 1
3, 6

page 17
1. a. fourth
   b. third
   c. first
   d. second
   e. Haley's
2. first: empty the wastebaskets
   second: take out the garbage
   third: wash the dishes
   fourth: dust her room

page 18
1. first
2. first
3. last
4. last
5. Next, last
6. First, Next, Last
7. first, Next, last
8. First, Next, last

page 19
Answers will vary.

page 20
1. 2, 3, 1, 4
2. 4, 1, 3, 2
3. 3, 4, 1, 2

4. 5, 1, 3 ,2 ,4
5. 2, 5, 4, 1, 3

page 21
• The sun's heat turns water into vapor.
• The warm vapor rises and begins to cool.
• The cooled vapor changes into water droplets.
• Billions of water droplets form a cloud.
• Water falls from the clouds as rain or snow.

spring, summer, fall

Answers will vary.

page 22
1. A baby kangaroo is called a *joey*.
2. Bears hibernate in the winter.
3. H20 is the symbol for water.
4. Vegetarians do not eat meat.
5. Olympic athletes hope to win gold medals.
6. Alaska is the land of the midnight sun.
7. Chicago is known as the Windy City.
8. Pike's Peak is 14,110 feet high.
9. Neil Armstrong was the first astronaut to walk on the moon.
10. A marine biologist studies animals and plants (or plants and animals) that live in water.

page 23
1. dinner or supper
2. Answers will vary.
3. before the movie starts
4. breakfast
5. Answers will vary.
6. no
7. no
8. clean the garage
9. Answers will vary.

10. Answers will vary.
11. Answers will vary.
12. Answers will vary.
13. math, science, social studies
14. finish my assignment
    help clean the fish tank
15. three, five, right

page 24
1. last
2. went to the parade
   went to the gas station
   picked up a prescription
       at the drugstore
3. first
   no
4. after the team played
5. Chuck
   Chuck's dad
6. at night
7. at noon
8. in the morning

page 25
Answers will vary.

page 26
Answers will vary.

page 27
Answers will vary.

page 28
1. late
2. Earlier: Max
   Later: Tyler
3. First: Kevin
   Second: Joan
   Third: Joan's parents
   Fourth: Joan's sister
4. 1:00 p.m.
5. 11:00 p.m.

page 29
1. Friday, Wednesday
2. Saturday, Sunday
3. Sunday, Saturday
4. yes
5. no, no
6. yes
7. no, yesterday

8. no, tomorrow

Situations and questions will vary.

page 30
1. Labor Day, first half
2. Tuesday
3. Wednesday
4. School Play
5. beginning
6. Open House
7. Varsity Football Game
8. School Play
9. Varsity Football Game
10. Friday

page 31
1. January, February, March,
   April, May, June, July, August,
   September, October,
   November, December
2. Answers will vary.
3. December, 1986
4. May, 1984
5. October
6. June 2005
7. April 2008
8. August
9. March
10. June, July, August
11. once a year
12. 12

page 32
1. no
2. no
3. Algebra I at 8:00, Computers
   at 9:00, Music at 10:00, and
   Sports Fitness at 11:00
4. 7:30
5. 6:30

page 33
Answers will vary.

■ ■ ■ Cause & Effect

page 38
1. Mark an **X** on the picture with
   a tornado in the background.

2. Mark an **X** on the picture
   showing a bouquet of
   flowers on the desk.

page 39
1. Mark an **X** on the skateboard
   ramp with a higher incline.
2. Mark an **X** on the boy studying.

page 40
1. The water overflowed.
   Circle the picture on the right.
   The person put too many
       ice cubes in the glass.
2. There's lots of hair in the drain.
   Circle the picture in the middle.
   The girl has long hair.

page 41
1. b
2. a
3. a
4. b
5. a

page 42
1. f
2. d
3. g
4. h
5. b
6. e
7. c
8. a

page 43
1. g
2. c
3. a
4. h
5. d
6. f
7. b
8. e

page 44
1. The person might get mad
   at you.
2. You might not be able to
   check out any more books.
3. You might get in trouble.

Answer Key, cont.

4. You might hurt someone's feelings.
5. You might get a bad grade.
6. You might not get credit for it.
7. You might not have anything to wear.
8. If someone finds out, you might get in trouble too.
9. The person might get cancer.
10. You might get a speeding ticket.
11. The electricity might go out and you'd lose what you're working on.
12. You might burn whatever you're baking.
13. You might have sore muscles.
14. You might get electrocuted.
15. You might damage your hearing.
16. You might get hit by a car.
17. You might take an incorrect dosage.
18. You might not get an exact time.

page 45
2. Karen was afraid to walk alone at night because of (the recent) (attacks on joggers)
3. Cal decided not to wash his car because (the forecast) (called for rain)
4. Jane didn't know what time it was because (she forgot to) (wear her watch to the store)
5. (Andy was sick on Friday) so he missed getting his math assignment.
6. (Kathryn didn't look at a map) (before her trip) and she got lost.
7. Mr. MacIntosh took his dog, Bear, to the vet because (Bear wasn't eating)
8. (Madison stopped eating) (candy and ice cream) and lost ten pounds.
9. Sean felt lonely after (the) (death of his grandfather)

10. (Leah decided to clean the) (inside of her car) so her friends would stop making fun of her.

page 46
1. Mark noticed his gas gauge was on E.
2. Jill would be eating dinner soon.
3. The weather was nice.
4. The Franklin's dog had been running away when it was outside.
5. It was raining.
6. The batteries were dead.
7. Morgan forgot to water her plant.
8. Someone planted flowers in Mrs. Lassiter's yard.

page 47
1. Cause: You put water in the freezer.
   Effect: The water freezes and makes ice.
2. Cause: You drop an egg.
   Effect: The egg breaks.
3. Cause: You eat too much.
   Effect: You are sick.
4. Cause: A tree limb falls on your house.
   Effect: Your roof is damaged.
5. Cause: The wind blew.
   Effect: There are leaves all over your yard.
6. Cause: You don't drink enough fluids.
   Effect: You become dehydrated.

page 48
1. Cause: There was no electricity.
   Effect: School was cancelled.
2. Cause: Craig ran over a nail.
   Effect: Craig's tire was flat.
3. Cause: Jarod had an argument with his friend.
   Effect: Jarod was sad.
4. Cause: Elliott finished running.
   Effect: Elliott was tired.

5. Cause: Claire got home late.
   Effect: Claire was in trouble.
6. Cause: It rained.
   Effect: Mackenzie didn't have to water the grass.

page 49
1. you might be tired the next day
2. you might cut your foot
3. you might not be able to see well
4. you might get a ticket/arrested
5. you might get a detention
6. your dog might get overweight
7. you might get cavities
8. you might waste water
9. your feet might get cold/wet
10. you might get bad breath
11. it might not turn out
12. an animal might get into it

page 50
1. People will laugh.
2. People won't want to be your friend.
3. The world will start to look like a garbage dump.
4. Something might get broken.
5. You might get in trouble.
6. You might get a good grade.
7. Your friend might say thank you.
8. People will want to be your friend.
9. You will help someone.
10. You might hurt the person's feelings.

page 51
1. It is raining hard.
   A water pipe broke.
   A fire hydrant is leaking.
2. There is a tornado warning.
   There has been an accident.
   There is a fire somewhere.
3. Your water heater is broken.
   Someone used all the hot water.
   You only turned on the cold water.

4. The store is sold out of those jeans.
   The store doesn't sell those jeans anymore.
   The jeans are in a different location in the store.
5. The TV is unplugged.
   The TV is broken.
   The electricity is off.

page 52
The second cause and effect will vary for each item.

2. <u>Certain chemicals might explode</u> if (you mix them)
3. (Doing nice things for people) <u>makes them happy</u>.
4. <u>You will be punished</u> (if you break the law)
5. (Taking a hot shower) <u>relaxes you</u>.
6. <u>You take medicine</u> (if you are sick)
7. (Eating salty foods) <u>makes you thirsty</u>.
8. (Large crowds) <u>make some people uncomfortable</u>.

page 53
wind – fly a kite, turn a windmill, make leaves fall from the trees, make waves on a lake or ocean
fear – stomach ache, cry, scream, tremble
earthquake – earth shakes, damage to buildings, people killed, fear
limited food supply – hungry people, dying people, fighting, food drive

page 54
1. d
2. h
3. a
4. c
5. f
6. b
7. g
8. e

page 55
Student additions to the lists will vary.

1. heavy snowstorms in winter, lots of melting snow in spring, flooding
2. high temperatures and humidity, turn on air conditioner, use more energy
3. children play outdoor sports, more laundry, increased water use, higher water bills
4. large sunny yard, hot in the house, planting shade trees, cooler temperature inside

page 56
Causes and effects will vary.

1. **American Cancer Society**
   provides research, education, advocacy, and service in an attempt to eliminate cancer as a major health problem
2. **American Red Cross**
   provides relief to victims of disasters and helps people prevent, prepare for, and respond to emergencies
3. **Humane Society**
   provides care for all lost, abandoned, abused, neglected, and unwanted companion animals; helps these animals find caring pet owners

page 57
Causes and effects will vary.

1. **Greenhouse Effect**
   the rise in temperature on Earth caused by certain gases in the atmosphere trapping energy from the sun
2. **Ultraviolet Rays**
   part of the electromagnetic spectrum emitted by the sun
3. **Mirage**
   an illusion in which an object that is seen at a distance is not really there

page 58
Possible causes and effects for each passage are provided together.

1. hard to find incuts/had trouble knowing where to put their hands and feet, finding incuts became too difficult/Clint and Joe rappelled to the ground
2. the squeeze is too narrow/Betsy's father can't get through, the squeeze is too narrow/they have to leave the cave or find a different route
3. Betsy and her father enter a dark zone/they use flashlights to see, Betsy and her father use their flashlights in a dark zone/they move through the cave safely

page 59
Possible causes and effects for each passage are provided together.

1. have a strong and experienced guide/travel down the river safely, take instruction on safety procedures/know how to paddle and what to do in an emergency
2. water flows through narrower areas of land/rapids, water in rapids is rough/rapids are hard to maneuver, water is rough/fall out of the raft, lifejacket is securely fastened/you are safe
3. watch cars racing around a track/get a thrill, favorite driver starts in pole position/fan gets excited, driver earns the fastest qualifying time/driver starts in pole position, driver starts in pole position/driver has a better chance of winning the race

page 60
Cause: First-Mart is open 24 hours a day.
Effect: Customers can shop at First-Mart anytime.

Cause: First-Mart has supply lists from all local schools.
Effect: Parents know what school supplies to purchase.

Cause: First-Mart has the lowest prices in town.
Effect: People who want to save money will shop at First-Mart.

page 61
Answers will vary.

■ ■ ■ Problem Solving

page 66
1. Circle the safety pin.
2. Mark an **X** on the cap.
3. Underline the boy sleeping.

page 67
1. Underline the tape.
2. Mark an **X** on the water bottle.
3. Circle the puppy.

page 68
1. The woman can't reach the light to change the bulb.
2. The shelf is already full and something might fall off if she tries to put the picture on it too.
3. The fire engine is caught in a traffic jam and can't get to the fire.
4. It will take time to fix the flat tire and the frozen foods might melt.

page 69
1. Mark an **X** on the picture on the right.

2. Circle the picture on the right.
3. Underline the picture on the left.

page 70
Answers are given for what the problems are. Answers will vary for what each person should do.

1. Mrs. Welch can't go outside to take care of her yard.
2. Kelly's car broke down.
3. Jack can't wash his hands because the sink is clogged.
4. A rabbit is eating the plants.

page 71
1. phone book
2. encyclopedia
3. dictionary
4. atlas
5. table of contents
6. cookbook
7. calendar
8. newspaper

page 72
1. electronics store
2. library
3. newspaper
4. police station
5. doctor's office
6. video store
7. antique store
8. art gallery

page 73
Answers are given for what the problems are. Answers will vary for what each person could do.

1. The pharmacy is closed.
2. The moving van is full.
3. The girl wore the wrong uniform.
4. The woman has too many things to carry.

page 74
Answers are given for what the problems are. Answers will vary for what could have prevented the problems from happening.

1. The hose is leaking.
2. The dog is getting loose because the fence is broken.
3. There's no wheelchair ramp.
4. The girl can't study because the music is too loud.

page 75
1. The movie was sold out. They went to a different movie. Answers will vary.
2. Blake's friends borrowed lunch money but never paid him back. He stopped bringing money to school. Answers will vary.
3. Connie needed to earn half of the money it cost to go on her class trip. She got a job. Answers will vary.

page 76
Answers will vary.

page 77
Answers are given for what the problems are. Solutions will vary.

1. You can't take the cat on vacation with you.
2. Your friends want you to go to the water park, but you can't swim very well.
3. There's a long line at the restaurant you want to eat at.
4. You're both too young to see the movie you were going to see.

page 78
Answers will vary.

page 79
Answers will vary.

page 80
1. helps prevent drownings
2. helps people see in the dark
3. protects cuts
4. detects fires
5. puts out fires
6. helps prevent bad breath/cavities
7. helps prevent accidents
8. helps prevent sunburns

page 81
Answers will vary.

page 82
1. It prevents people from talking at the same time so the speaker can be heard.
2. It helps prevent you from doing the assignment incorrectly.
3. It helps prevent you from facing a possibly dangerous situation.
4. It prevents you from having to tell a stranger that you're home alone.
5. It prevents your pet from running away.
6. It helps prevent accidents.
7. It prevents your family from worrying about you.
8. It prevents you from falling out or getting hurt on the ride.

page 83
1. Camping so near a cliff with two small children and a dog could be dangerous.

   The family could have called ahead or arrived earlier at the camp to get a better campsite.
2. The lot and the abandoned building could be a dangerous place to play.

   The boys could find somewhere else to play.

3. They won't be able to find a good parking spot.

   They could go to the mall another day.

page 84
Answers will vary.

page 85
Answers will vary.

page 86
Answers will vary.

page 87
Answers will vary.

page 88
Missing information:
ticket prices, where to purchase tickets/phone number, location of the concert, who's performing

Advertisements will vary.

page 89
Answers will vary.

■ ■ ■ Opinions

Answers will vary for all items in this unit, except the following.

page 101
1. Opinion
2. Opinion
3. Fact
4. Fact
5. Opinion
6. Fact
7. Opinion
8. Opinion
9. Opinion
10. Fact

page 102
1. Opinion
2. Fact
3. Opinion
4. Opinion
5. Opinion
6. Opinion
7. Opinion
8. Opinion
9. Fact
10. Fact
11. Fact
12. Opinion

page 103
1. Fact
2. Opinion
3. Opinion
4. Fact
5. Fact
6. Opinion
7. Opinion
8. Fact
9. Fact
10. Opinion
11. Fact
12. Opinion

page 116
Circle:
Terrific Tanning Gel
For a more natural look
Better than tanning beds!

■ ■ ■ Inferencing

Answers may vary for several of these activities. Accept any reasonable responses, provided the student gives a logical response to the item and backs it up with appropriate reasoning. Suggested answers have been provided for the following pages.

page 122
1. Circle the picture on the left.
2. Circle the picture on the left.
3. Circle the picture on the right.

page 123
1. Mark an **X** on the picture on the left.
2. Mark an **X** on the picture on the right.
3. Mark an **X** on the picture on the left.

page 124
1. Point to the picture in the middle.
2. Point to the picture in the middle.
3. Point to the picture on the left.

page 125
1. The person is a veterinarian.
2. The person is a teacher.
3. The person likes to cook/bake or The person is a chef/baker.
4. The person likes to paint or The person is an artist.

page 126
1. dog
2. shocking/disturbing message
3. hot
4. scary

page 127
1. drum
2. egg
3. backpack or bookbag
4. envelope
5. bicycle
6. ambulance
7. elephant
8. turtle
9. vehicle
10. computer
11. train
12. newspaper

page 128
1. swimming pool
2. castle
3. jungle or forest
4. garden
5. airport, bus station, train station
6. racetrack

7. The Statue of Liberty
8. Mount Rushmore
9. Answers will vary.
10. Answers will vary.

page 129
1. janitor or cleaning person
2. pediatrician
3. carpenter
4. judge
5. office worker
6. mechanic

page 134
1. a
2. b
3. b
4. a
5. b
6. b
7. b
8. a

page 136
1. get his dad something to drink
2. mow the grass
3. clean up the kitchen
4. stop reading and pick up her things
5. tell his girlfriend goodbye and get off the phone
6. help her

page 138
1. WON: Bulldogs
   LOST: Greyhounds
2. WON: Knights
   LOST: Spartans
3. WON: Giants
   LOST: Miners
4. WON: Rangers
   LOST: Tigers
5. WON: Iowa
   LOST: Wisconsin
6. WON: Ravens
   LOST: Hawks
7. WON: Lakers
   LOST: Twisters
8. WON: Groundhogs
   LOST: Rattlers

page 139
1. Let's get ready to hear the sports scores.
2. Para hit a home run and scored one run.
3. Roland finally got a hit.
4. The Vikings and the Bears will play tonight.
5. The Blue's pitcher is giving up a lot of hits.
6. If Ryan gets on base we're sure to score a run because he's so fast.
7. The Spirit has been unable to score a point.
8. Zimmerman's kick won the championship game for the Racers.
9. Miller had a good putt.
10. The Cubs won one game and the Cardinals won the other.

■ ■ ■ Paraphrasing

page 150
1. bug
2. step
3. dirt
4. street
5. café
6. janitor
7. pal
8. hat
9. chef
10. rug
11. pupil
12. physician

page 151
1. huge
2. close
3. little
4. skinny
5. wet
6. mix
7. angry
8. tardy
9. pop
10. sleep

181

11. sick
12. talk
13. loud
14. happy
15. end
16. picture
17. fun
18. jump
19. round
20. show

page 152
1. a
2. b
3. a
4. a
5. b
6. a
7. b
8. a

page 153
1. a
2. b
3. a
4. b
5. a
6. a
7. b
8. a

page 154
1. relatives
2. furniture
3. appliances
4. tools
5. jewelry
6. sciences
7. trees
8. writing utensils
9. transportation
10. currency

page 155
1. expensive
2. Dissolve
3. migrated
4. hibernate
5. diagram
6. decrease
7. increase

8. finish
9. ancestors
10. island

page 156
Sentences will vary.

2. small rock
3. dense forest
4. huge boat
5. fast children
6. luxury auto
7. ripped jacket
8. smart instructor
9. funny movie
10. middle chair

page 157
Sentences will vary.

1. wander the forest
2. scary show
3. hate bugs
4. empty space
5. great escape
6. many thoughts
7. well-known writer
8. brief remark
9. most recent events
10. bad scent

page 158
Sentences will vary.

2. boring group of people
3. tastes awful
4. many pages
5. yearly event
6. extra tire
7. horse was a winner
8. successful attorney
9. brave soldier
10. under the surface

page 159
1. No
2. No
3. No
4. Yes
5. No
6. No

7. Yes
8. No
9. Yes
10. Yes
11. Yes
12. No
13. Yes
14. No
15. No
16. No
17. Yes
18. Yes

page 160
1. on time
2. breaks easily
3. frightened
4. small
5. tired
6. driving over the speed limit
7. still
8. ugly
9. funny
10. old
11. does both things at the same time
12. excited
13. naughty
14. difficult

page 161
2. were crooked; Mrs. Sellers repainted the stripes because they were crooked.
3. did refuse; The Crawford's did refuse the package from the UPS driver.
4. was right; Corrine challenged the teacher about her test grade because she knew her answer was right.
5. was false; Chris was surprised when she heard the news because she knew the report was false.
6. was innocent; Carson recognized the man on the front page of the newspaper. He knew the man was innocent.

Answer Key, cont.

page 162
1. **Many** reptiles are land animals. However, many groups of reptiles can also **live** in the water.
2. The cheetah is an **interesting** mammal. This **pretty** animal is a daytime hunter. The cheetah is very **fast**, running at speeds up to 70 mph.
3. Did you know a chameleon is **particularly** well-suited to **living** in bushes and trees? Its body is **wide**, giving it **steadiness** when climbing.
4. Lizards are interesting creatures. **Many** lizards **create** eggs with leathery shells. Lizards are **hardly ever** attentive to their eggs once they are laid.
5. Garret and Nathan **enjoy** going to the zoo with their **relatives**. They **like** watching the **gigantic** elephants **do** tricks. They always **run** to the monkey house.

page 163
Answers will vary.

page 164
Answers will vary.

page 165
Answers will vary.

page 166
2. I don't need your advice at all.
3. Marcie was afraid she'd fail when she tried out for the play.
4. Allen didn't mean to offend anyone when he changed the plan.
5. Most students thought the test was hard, but Tiana thought it was easy.
6. Elijah's parents were very upset when he wasn't home by 10:00 p.m.
7. Chelsey smiled because she knew she had played a trick on her brother.
8. Jay knew that it would be difficult to find enough extra costumes for the play by next Friday.

page 167
2. I'm so tired. I'm going home to rest.
3. Go ahead, you know what to do.
4. With the river on the rise, volunteers worked 24 hours a day filling sandbags.
5. The team is ready to go!
6. The police were concerned because someone gave the names to the press.
7. My mom got very upset when she heard what happened after the game.

8. Chuck took the blame for someone else's actions.
9. It's a delicate situation. We really have to take care with this one.
10. Sherrie was worried that the volunteers would leave and she would be the only one at the Hunger Drive.

page 168
Sentences will vary.

2. get up in a bad mood
3. very clean
4. confusing
5. irritate me
6. could become a problem
7. very bored
8. get organized

page 169
Answers will vary.

page 170
Answers will vary.

page 171
Answers will vary.

page 172
Answers will vary.

page 173
Answers will vary.

19-05-98765432